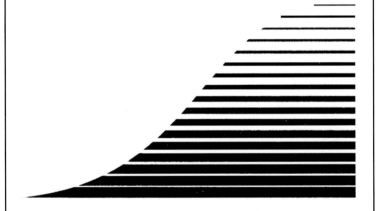

FUNDAMENTALS OF

Project

Performance

Measurement

Robert R. Kemps

Humphreys & Associates, Inc.

Management Consultants

3111 N. Tustin Avenue, Suite 120

Orange, CA 92865

(714) 685-1730   http://www.humphreys-assoc.com

DIRECT ALL REORDERS TO
HUMPHREYS & ASSOCIATES, INC.

Revised 1996
Revised 2000
Revised 2004

Humphreys & Associates, Inc.
Management Consultants
3111 N. Tustin Avenue, Suite 120
Orange, CA 92865
(714) 685-1730
http://www.humphreys-assoc.com

Library of Congress Catalog-in-Publication Data

Kemps, Robert R. (Robert Raynier), 1934-
      Fundamentals of Project Performance Measurement /
   by Robert R. Kemps.
         p. cm
         Includes Index.
         ISBN 0-912495-21-9
         1. Industrial Project Management.
         2. Industrial Development Projects--Evaluation.
         I. Title
HD69.P75K456   1992
858.4'04--dc20

2 3 4 5 6 7 8 9 0

Fundamentals of
Project Performance Measurement

...explains the important elements of *project cost/schedule management* in a concise and straightforward way without falling back on the jargon often associated with the subject.

...emphasizes the use of the *earned value technique* as a logical and meaningful way to present cost and schedule status for management and estimating purposes.

...is profusely illustrated, numerous examples are used to clarify concepts and cogent reasons are given for why management systems should possess specific capabilities.

Here is a text that can be read and understood easily; a rarity in today's complex management environment.

Table of Contents

List of Figures

Preface

This book is an excellent place to start for those who wish to learn more about project performance measurement and will be useful to representatives of each of the disciplines that contribute to the success of a project. A clear understanding of the fundamentals of project performance measurement is essential to effective project management. However, this understanding is as essential for managers and staff that must use the project management system on a daily basis as it is for higher level managers and their customers. It is an engineering axiom that the better a process can be measured, the better it can be controlled. In *Fundamentals of Project Performance Measurement*, Bob Kemps teaches us that project performance is no exception.

Project Performance Measurement, once a little known and poorly understood project management process, has now become a way of life throughout the R&D, Production and Construction communities. Argument that once raged over whether it could be done at all, now focus on how best to use the data from established performance measurement systems. Individuals once responsible for introducing performance measurement systems, often in the face of considerable opposition, are responsible for managing entire projects. Project managers that have not learned the value of these systems are finding themselves at a considerable disadvantage, not only in dealing with internal and external competition for increasingly scarce resources, but also in satisfying the needs of increasingly knowledgeable customers.

High ranking government officials can speak with ease of the output of performance measurement systems and have done so in televised congressional hearings. The governments of Australia, Canada, Sweden and Japan, among others, are showing increasing interest in establishing performance measurement standards; and some are surpassing the United States in the quality of the implementation of those standards. Commercial enterprises at home and abroad are adopting performance measurement systems for themselves in response to market pressure to do a better job of managing projects. Even Government agencies that are seeking to free their managers and contractors of some of the strict discipline of cost/schedule planning and controls continue to recognize the value of performance measurement systems.

It is against this background that Bob Kemps' primer on project performance measurement comes to us. He calls upon his many years in the field to remind us that despite the contribution that performance measurement systems have made to the art of project management, and despite the regard those systems have won for their users, there is no magic here. *Fundamentals of Project Performance Measurement* explains in simple terms the underlying concepts that combine to create the sound systems that produce the data so essential to the cost, schedule, and technical trade-offs of the project manager's craft. This book treats as especially important the process of combining those simple concepts and does not allow us to fall victim to the belief that it can be done easily and without the involved contributions of the entire project team or, as Bob would say, without discipline.

Gary C Humphreys
Humphreys & Associates, Inc.

CHAPTER

Introduction

An important part of the project management is the art of making trade-offs – trading off cost, schedule, and technical performance in an effort to get the best product at the lowest cost in the shortest time. Performance measurement, on the other hand, is the art of determining, organizing, and presenting cost, schedule, and technical performance information in a way that contributes to making those trade-offs. Good Performance measurement requires the effective integration of cost, schedule, and technical information. Unfortunately, many management systems that are used on large projects are not well integrated because they were developed independently of each other to satisfy specific needs. For example, the accounting system is designed primarily to keep track of expenses and payments, to meet payrolls, calculate taxes, ect. Cost Information is primarily oriented to organizational elements. The scheduling system, on the other hand, is designed to support work planning and control, and is oriented to project tasks. Technical management is focused on specifications, performance characteristics, and technical goals, and is a product of the system engineering process.

Pulling Essential cost, schedule, and technical information together in a meaningful, coherent fashion is always a challenge facing a project manager. If this cannot be done, management information will be fragmented, will not contribute effectively to project management, and may actually mislead the manager by presenting a distorted view of project status.

In the simplest terms, performance measurement is the comparison of actual performance against a baseline plan. The baseline used for performance measurement should be a single, integrated plan, because the analysis of cost performance must include schedule considerations and the evaluation of schedule performance must include technical performance considerations. Figure 1-1 illustrates the difficulty in trying to understand cost performance separately based on a commonly used budget versus actual presentation.

At first glance, it would appear that the project is in good shape from a cost standpoint. The chart seems to indicate that cost performance is better than planned and that an underrun is likely. Suppose, though, that the project is behind schedule. When this fact is taken in to consideration, it is not clear that the variance between budget and actual costs represents good cost performance or simply the fact that work is not getting done. The problem with the chart is that it compares apples to oranges. It compares the Actual

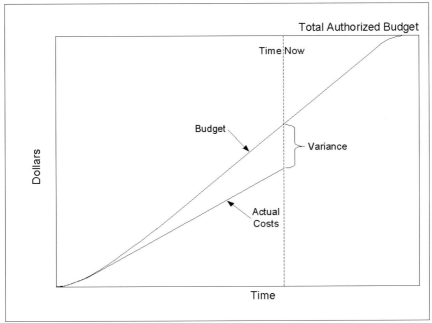

Figure **1-1**: Project Cost Report

Cost of Work Performed (ACWP) to the Budgeted Cost for Work Scheduled (BCWS). What is missing is the Budgeted Cost for Work Performed (BCWP), commonly referred to as Earned Value.

When earned value is taken into consideration, the cost picture clears up because the cost and schedule components can be addressed separately. Figure 1-2 illustrates the variance attributable to cost performance and the variance attributable to schedule performance.

The chart now shows that the project is both behind schedule and underrunning cost, and the cost underrun is only about half that depicted in Figure 1-1. Earned value is the key to understanding project status because it represents the amount of work performed. In developing an estimate

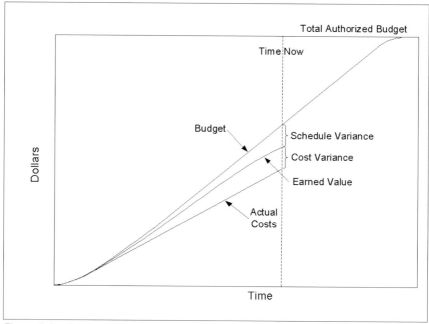

Figure **1-2**: Cost/Schedule Performance

of the final project cost, earned value also provides the point of departure for determining the amount of work remaining.

As with cost performance measurement, schedule performance cannot be fully evaluated by itself. Technical problems, such as test failures or performance shortfalls, are responsible for most schedule and cost problems; consequently, technical performance cannot be ignored, as problems may not surface until too late to take effective action. However, most cost and schedule control systems operate on the *assumption* that technical requirements are being met when credit is taken for work accomplished. This is not always the case and an early warning system of technical performance measurement helps to identify potential sched-

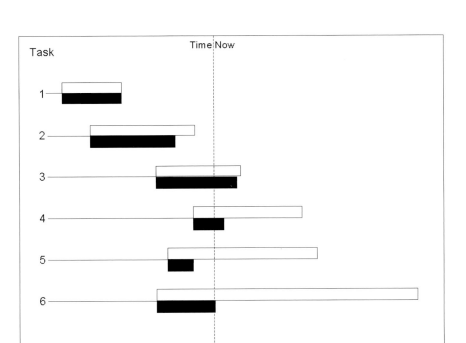

Figure **1-3**:   Project Schedule

ule and cost problems and their impact on project objectives.

Schedule reports do not always present a clear picture of project status even though a variety of indicators may be provided, such as tasks completed, milestones accomplished, tasks ahead of schedule, task behind schedule, float available, etc. In many cases, however, there is no bottom line that indicates the project is "x" number of days ahead or behind schedule.

Figure 1-3 illustrates a situation where some tasks are on schedule, some are ahead of schedule, and some are behind schedule, making overall project status virtually impossible to determine.

Another problem is that firm schedule baselines can be difficult to maintain. Replanning activities tend to eliminate schedule variances by continually rescheduling project activities, including the work that has fallen behind schedule. Without a stable baseline, meaningful performance measurement cannot take place and performance trends cannot be ascertained. The same comment pertains to budget discipline. If budgets are to be used for measuring cost performance, the budget assigned to a task cannot be arbitrarily changed whenever it becomes apparent that the budget cannot be met. Even worse, if the added budget should be "borrowed" from downstream work, this robbing of Peter to pay Paul can delay visibility of cost problems until to late to do any thing about them other than to get more money. Chasing baseline changes is not a substitute for performance measurement.

Given the types of problems described above, it is no wonder that many project managers are flying by the seat of their pants without a good feel for where the project stands at any given point in time. This may not be to serious on small efforts, but on large projects, a project manager is constantly working a myriad of problems and cannot keep track of or figure out the cost of schedule impacts that individual problems are having on the project. A systematic, organized process for collecting performance information and presenting it in a clear manner on a regular basis is essential to the project management process. This book is intended to define the basic elements of an effective performance measurement system.

C H A P T E R

Understanding The Project

Project planning is not easy! The larger the project, the more difficult it is, particularly where a large amount of development activity is involved. It is not unusual to see projects falling behind schedule in the early stages for a variety of reasons, one of which is that the effort required to plan the project and establish the baseline is often underestimated. It takes time to define the work and develop a realistic project baseline; and it requires the involvement of key people who have the necessary experience to do it right, which means those other people are not going to be available to do other things.

Project planning is iterative. Doing step two often means redoing step one. Each progressive step brings new considerations and new limitations. A wonderful schedule plan that cannot be supported by available resources is not a good schedule because it cannot be carried out.

The first step in the planning process is gaining an understanding of the full scope of the project. Schedules

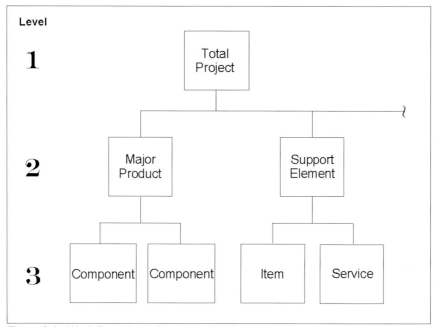

Figure **2-1**: Work Breakdown Structure (WBS)

cannot be developed until the work tasks have been defined and participating organizations have been identified.

A useful device to aid in defining the work is a Work Breakdown Structure (WBS). A WBS looks like a typical company organization chart, but it is a breakdown of the products and services that constitute the project rather than the organizations that will do the work. It is often described as a product-oriented family tree and looks like the illustration in figure 2-1.

The top block of the WBS represents the total project; thus, it includes all the work required to complete the project. It would not be rational to claim that something was left out of the WBS since the entire project is wrapped up in the block at level one. Level two of the WBS is usually segregates the primary project to be developed, produced or constructed from supporting elements and services, such as project management, data, systems engineering, and support equipment. Level three further divides the level-two elements into their component parts and services. This progressive subdivision continues until the work has been defined to a manageable degree; that is, increments of work have been identified that are considered suitable for assigning management responsibility for their accomplishment. The determination of what constitutes a managerially significant unit of work is based on experience, scope and complexity of work, risk, visibility, and other factors relevant to the project. In summary, the WBS is a systematic approach to ensuring that all the project work is recognized and defined so it can be developed in to a viable work plan. The idea is to fully understand what has to be done to carry out the project. Therefore, the WBS elements must be described in enough detail not only to ensure that all the work has been identified, but to eliminate duplication and overlap where the same work seems to appear in different places. These descriptions make up a WBS dictionary that defines the work explicitly and provides a basis for control of scope changes during the life of the project.

While the initial purpose of WBS is to help define the project work, once in place it provides a useful framework for integrating management subsystems and accumulating performance information. Disconnects and mismatches between systems can be minimized if estimates, budgets, schedules, costs, accomplishments, and projections are all oriented to a common structure. The WBS can serve this purpose. In a contractual situation, the customer often purposes a summary level structure that ultimately serves as the

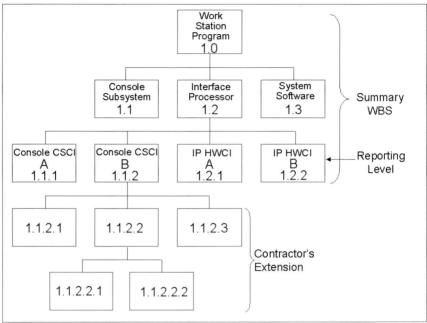

Figure **2-2**: Contract Work Breakdown Structure (CWBS)

framework for reporting on the contract. The contractor extends the summary structure in accordance with the way the work will be done. The entire WBS is then referred to as the Contract WBS (CWBS).

The customer's summary WBS is usually designed to satisfy specific data collection needs, perhaps because there is a desire to track certain components or subsystems, or in order to support cost estimating data bases. By delineating specific elements of the WBS, collection of the information for those elements is facilitated. In most cases, there is a flexibility for adjusting the customer-specified summary WBS during the negotiation process to accommodate the way the contractor plans to do the work. Figure 2-2 illustrates the CWBS.

CHAPTER

Organizing For
The Project

As the Work Breakdown Structure identifies the work to be done, the Organization Breakdown Structure (OBS) identifies the people that will do the work. Figure 3-1 shows a representative OBS.

The OBS and WBS must be brought together before work plan can be formulated, schedules prepared and budgets allocated. The biggest challenge is determining the appropriate levels of work and organizational breakdown to effect this integration, because a management control point will be created that, to a large extent, will determine the cost and efficiency of the management system. For example, if the WBS is driven to a very low level of indenture and the OBS establishes management responsibility at a low organizational level, the marriage of the two structures can result in an extremely detailed management control system with excessive documentation and administrative processes. On the other hand, bringing the two structures together at too

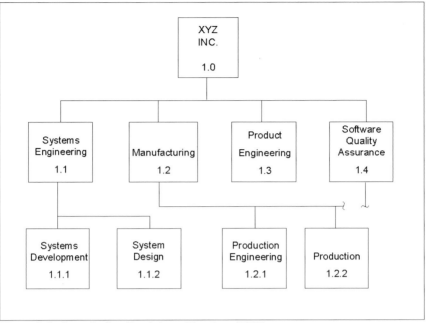

Figure **3-1**: Organization Breakdown Structure (OBS)

gross a level can result in a management system that is too loose; i.e. work elements may be too large, complex and ill-defined, and organizational responsibilities may not be well focused. Consequently, baseline discipline can be difficult to maintain because of the lack of work definition and the amount of replanning flexibility available within assigned areas of responsibility.

As previously mentioned, work planning is an iterative process; thus, finding the right levels of work definition and organizational responsibility, may require several iterations of the WBS and OBS that consider such factors as work scope, complexity, volume, cost, time duration, span of organization control, and other factors. Identifying the appropriate level is a judgement call that is based on experience with other projects and knowledge of what has worked and what has not worked.

Companies organize differently for different projects. A very large project that dominates the business base may foster an organizational structure that mirrors the project with virtually everyone reporting to the project manager. Many companies, though, have numerous projects that draw on established functional organizations through a matrix approach. Recently, more and more companies are moving into an environment that employs multifunctional work teams for work management and performance as opposed to traditional functional organizations. Regardless of how the organization is structured, responsibility for work must eventually be assigned, resources must be allocated and individuals held accountable for its accomplishment. The assignment of responsibility occurs at the point where organizational or work team involvement with a WBS element is identified. This point is often referred to as the control account level. Figure 3-2 illustrates the integration of the WBS with the OBS to form control accounts.

A definition for a control account could be that it represents one organization's effort on one WBS element. Control accounts can occur at various levels (but always below the lowest elements in the WBS), since the WBS indenture stops at whatever level represents a manageable unit of work. Obviously, large complex tasks require more levels of indenture than do supporting elements. For any given leg of the WBS, management must decide what constitutes a sufficient breakdown of work. The same logic pertains to the OBS, since some tasks can be managed at higher organizational levels than others. The objective is to establish enough con-

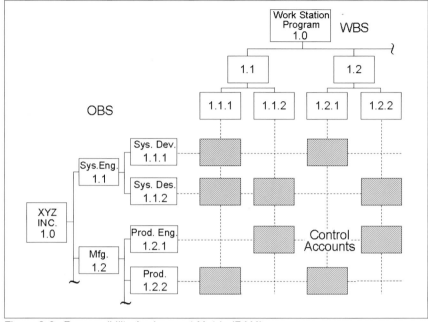

Figure **3-2**: Responsibility Assignment Matrix (RAM)

trol accounts to ensure good planning and control discipline and visibility, but not so many that the system becomes overly cumbersome and costly to operate.

A general rule of thumb applicable to the size of control accounts on a large project is that the time required for that work should run about a year in duration. The rationale for that concept is based on the trade-off between baseline discipline and management flexibility. The control account manager normally has the authority to replan work within the framework of the control account schedule and budget. This flexibility can only be provided within limits, and the one-year guideline seems to be a logical constraint in most environments. Without such a guideline, some other limitation on replanning may be necessary to preclude situations where budgets planned for downstream work are used to cover today's problems, sometimes reoffered to as the "rubber baseline" problem. Dollar amount and work complexity may also effect the size of control accounts.

It may not be possible or practical to plan the entire project to the control level at the outset. In such cases, planning may be carried only to an intermediate WBS level until more detailed planning can be accomplished. The primary consideration is that the work must be planned in enough detail to ensure that adequate resources are reserved for that work. If all of the work cannot be defined, it is possible to establish a realistic baseline for the entire project. Near-term work may have more budget Allocated than its fair share of the project budget before it becomes apparent that the project's budget is Front Loaded.

CHAPTER

Scheduling

When most people think about project planning and control, they usually think about scheduling. Once the project has been formally structured, the work has been defined and organizational responsibilities identified, the scheduling process can take place. Those who have tried to schedule a project without going through the preliminary phases, especially the WBS development, may find themselves with an incomplete project plan. Scheduling activity is not a substitute for the WBS. The WBS forces recognition and definition of all the effort involved in the project. Without a WBS, it is easy to ignore or overlook significant activities that must be accommodated in the overall project plan. The first step of in the development of a schedule is to recognize all the work that must be done. The WBS facilitates that process.

There are many different kinds of scheduling techniques, including milestone charts, Gantt charts, networks, Manufacturing Resource Planning (MRP), and combinations thereof. All have advantages and disadvantages depending on the type of project activity involved. Networking is often preferred for large, one-of-a-kind type projects, especially now that modern software and computer graphics have reduced the administrative burden associated with statusing and updating. Networking, however, is is not suited to repetitive manufacturing processes; rather, Manufacturing Resource Planning (MRP) would be more appropriate. The simplicity and ease of use of milestone and Gantt charts makes them appealing to many managers, but these techniques do not easily accommodate the complexities associated with interdependencies among activities.

The scheduling system selected for any project should have certain characteristics and capabilities. There must be a master schedule that lays out the total scope of the project from beginning to end and that includes key milestones and decision points designated by management or directed by the customer. In a contractual situation, schedule targets, technical review points, delivery dates, and other significant milestones are negotiated or directed. For internal projects, company management establishes the schedule targets. Failure to do so results in an open-ended project that cannot be effectively baselined or managed. Goal-setting is an essential part of project management; and it is surprising how many times it is not properly done, particularly in the research and development or laboratory environment.

The master schedule is the summary-level schedule baseline for the project. it should be relatively static with changes resulting only from contractual modifications or deliberate management decisions. Updating and revising the project master schedule because of an inability to perform the work should not be permitted on a routine basis, although work-arounds to accommodate problems should be displayed. Yet, many schedule practitioners allow such changes to occur and, consequently, a firm schedule baseline is not maintained. Instead, the schedule is continually being redrawn every time performance is reported, causing the original baseline to be discarded and, in effect, preempting the schedule management process. The efficient software that facilitates schedule maintenance sometimes contributes to this problem if not properly implemented.

Detail-level schedules are needed to manage the work. There cannot, however, be a disconnect between the detail-level schedules and the master schedule. Consequently, there may also be a series of intermediate-level schedules that link the detail to the summary levels. This linkage from top to bottom is sometimes referred to as vertical traceability. The sequencing of activities from beginning to end of the project that recognizes interdependencies between tasks is referred to as horizontal traceability. Maintaining both vertical and horizontal traceability is essential if the scheduling system is to be an effective management tool. Figure 4-1 illustrates the concept of vertical traceability.

As mentioned earlier, the control account is a key management control point because of responsibility for work accomplishment is established at that level. The control account is a defined element of work to be preformed by a specific organizational entity. It will have a described scope of work, a schedule, and a budget. The control account manager plans the detailed work tasks, manages their accomplishment, and reports regularly to the project manager. The detail-level schedule often takes the form of control account planning sheet since work packages and tasks must support

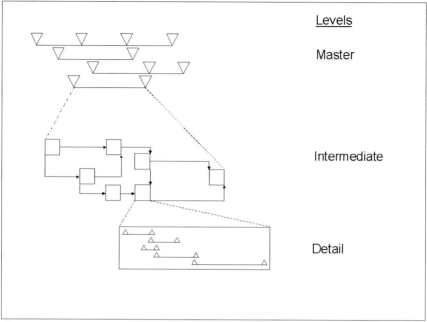

Figure **4-1**: Schedule Vertical Traceability

control account work requirements, and because systems integration occurs at the control account level.

Schedule preparations may cause another iteration of the WBS resulting in the addition or deletion of WBS elements as viable work plans evolve. But once schedules are established for the control accounts, schedule data for higher level WBS or organizational elements can be derived by simply summarizing control account data. Thus, there is no need to develop specific schedules for each WBS or organization element. If intermediate level schedules are developed, they do not need to equate to any specific WBS or organizational level. A logically developed WBS, however, tends to facilitate schedule development at certain levels to accommodate system, subsystem or component development, production, or construction.

CHAPTER 5

Budgeting

It has been said that good budgeting is the uniform distribution of dissatisfaction. A Performance Measurement System, currently referred to as an Earned Value Management System, is dependent on good budgeting practices to provide a realistic baseline against which actual costs can be compared. A fundamental requirement is that the internal budgets must add up to the project's Total Authorized Budget. That total budget is set by management as the cost goal for the project, and the project budget reflects a distribution of that goal to project activities. This is an allocation process, based on estimates generated during the project's conceptual phase, that results in each managerially significant element of work (control account) with an authorized budget that represents its value in terms of overall project. As the work is performed, the actual costs recorded for the work performed can be compared to its budgeted value to reflect cost performance. For a contract, the negotiated contract cost, exclusive for profit or fee, normally provides the point of departure for the budget baseline.

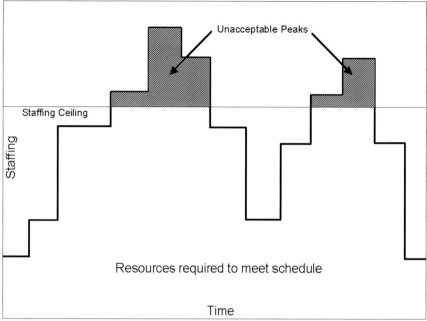

Figure **5-1**: Resource Leveling

It is common practice to set aside a budget for unforeseen work, problem resolution, and management control purposes, which is usually referred to as Management Reserve (MR). The amount of management reserve depends on several factors, including how well the company did in negotiations, the risk associated with the project because of complexity and uncertainty, and management judgment. The management reserve is the project manager's budget for the known unknowns. It gives the project manager flexibility to cope with problems or unexpected events because it provides a resource budget to apply as needed. Without a reserve, the project manager is unable to provide budgetary relief to lower level managers unless resources can be found by eliminating unneeded activities or achieving efficiencies in other areas. These opportunities are few and far between.

The remainder of the budget is authorized to the internal organizations assigned to perform the work. That work has already been scheduled, at least preliminarily, so the distribution of budget to scheduled increments of work produces a time-phased budget baseline for the project. Again, the process iterative in nature. The spread of resources to what appears to be an optimum schedule may reveal a plan that cannot be performed. This happens because resources cannot be turned on and off like a faucet. An initial resource-loaded schedule will have peaks and valleys that must be smoothed in order to maximize the efficient use of people, materials, and facilities. Resource leveling involves adjusting schedules and may not result in the earliest possible completion date, although contracted dates and targets set by management must be accommodated. Figure 5-1 shows the resource leveling process, the idea being to cut off the peaks and fill the valleys by rephrasing activities.

Internal budgets must address the direct and indirect (overhead) activities. Direct cost are managed at the control account level while indirect costs are usually managed at a more summary level in a pool arrangement. In addition, the budget planning must consider work which part of the project but which cannot be identified in the WBS or the OBS in detail at the onset. Budget must be set aside for that work to ensure it will not be incorrectly distributed before the work is incorporated into the correct control account(s). This undistributed budget is also part of the total budget baseline.

Figure 5-2 illustrates the elements that make up the project's budget.

Within the control account, budgets should be delineated

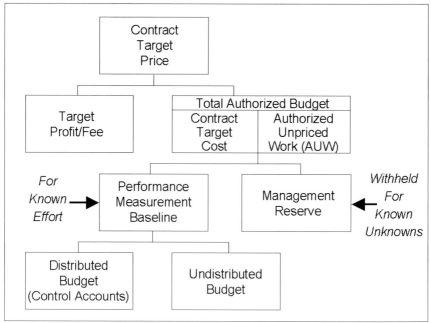

Figure **5-2**: Budget Allocation

in terms of major cost elements; i.e., labor, material, subcontracts, and other direct costs. Cost element segregation is necessary to accommodate the differences in management and control of these elements so that cost variances can be analyzed in those terms. Understanding how much of a problem is related to material costs and how much is related to labor performance is of considerable interest to the project manager, particularly when estimating costs for the work remaining.

CHAPTER 6

Establishing The Baseline

The performance measurement baseline (PMB) is the product of a planning process that involves identifying and defining the work, designating and assigning organizational responsibility for doing the work, scheduling the work tasks in accordance with established targets, and allocating budgets to the scheduled increments of work as shown in Figure 6-1.

Establishing the initial baseline for a large project is a difficult and time consuming effort, but it pays many dividends in terms of understanding the full scope of the project and being realistic about the job that lies ahead. Many costs overruns and schedule slippages on large projects are the result of not fully recognizing and, consequently, underestimating the scope and complexity of the work to be done. Without a comprehensive plan that realistically addresses the total project, the project may proceed on a basis of near-term plans without knowing whether resource consumption

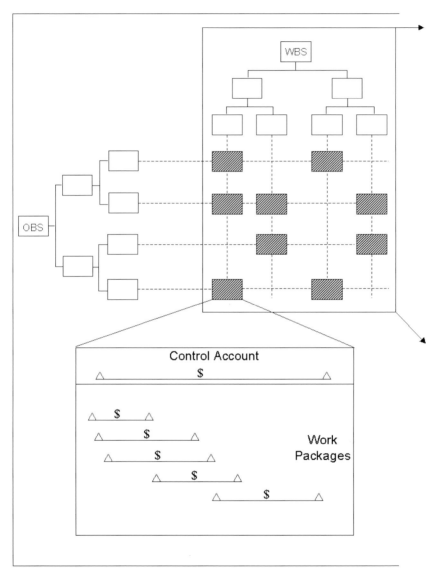

Figure **6-1**: Performance Measurement Baseline

is consistent with the equitable distribution of budget for the overall project. In other words, if the downstream work cannot be defined, there is no way to know that sufficient

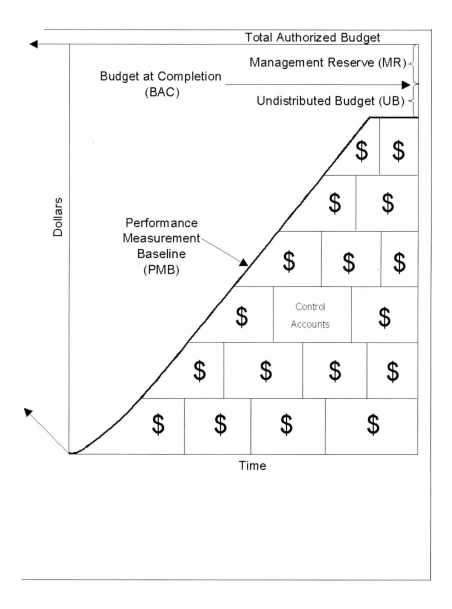

resources have been set aside for that work when the time comes to do it. Thus, the downstream surprise occurs when it finally becomes obvious that the good performance to

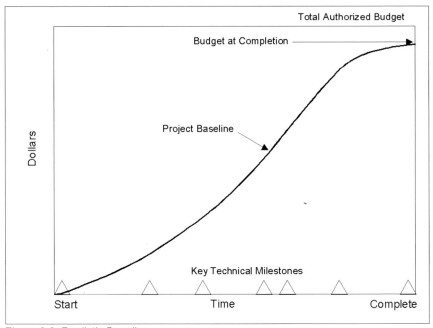

Figure **6-2**: Realistic Baseline

date has really been at the expense of the work remaining to be done.

The baseline must make sense. It must be logical. It must be rational. A good way to ensure the baseline is all of these is to look at the context; to actually plot the numbers, dollars against time, lay in the key technical and schedule milestones, and assess the realism of the resulting resource, or"S" curve. Figure 6-2 shows a typical baseline curve.

Evaluating the adequacy of the baseline is not as hard as it sounds. Once a certain level of resources; i.e., work force and facilities, are determined to be necessary to a project, costs will be incurred at a very predictable rate. After the initial build-up, the baseline plan should be almost a straight line up to the point where significant work force reductions can logically take place.

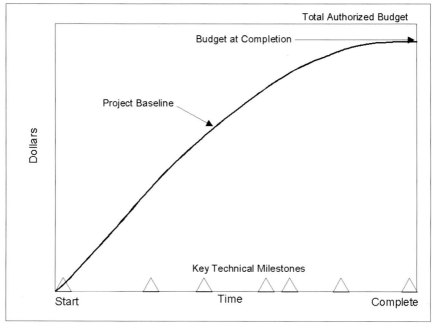

Figure **6-3**: Front Loaded Baseline

Looking at key technical and schedule milestones in con-junction with the baseline curve will provide some useful insights as to when manpower can logically be removed from the project. A baseline plan that indicates a tailing off of resources well before major milestones have been achieved is probably unrealistic and should be challenged. Figure 6-3 illustrates an apparent front-loaded baseline that would not seem, at first glance, to support the downstream work.

Another element that can affect the project baseline is the ability to fund that baseline plan. Many projects are incre-mentally funded, and a baseline plan cannot be established that ignores affordability constraints. Figure 6-4 illustrates a situation where incremental funding does not support the desired baseline plan. In this example, if the third and

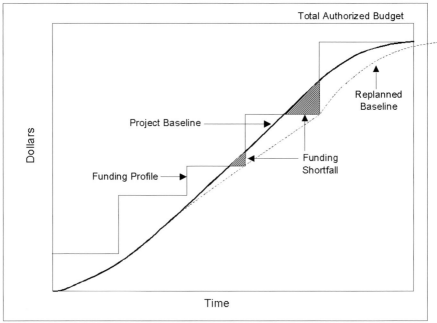

Figure **6-4**: Project Funding vs. The Baseline

fourth increments of funding cannot be increased, the project must be replanned to accommodate these constraints. Replanning will likely result in a stretchout of the project with a concomitant increase in the project cost.

Funding perturbations during the life of a project are a major cause of project cost and schedule problems. Every effort should be taken to ensure funding stability to the extent possible. External budgetary decisions made without regard to impacts on individual projects are often responsible for schedule slippages and cost overruns.

There is often confusion about the difference between project *funding* and performance *budgeting*. Funding the *real money*. The bills must be paid, including overruns. Funding must be made available, as required, by management for an internal project, or by the customer in a contractual situation. Various arrangements can be made to provide funds in the form of progress payments, payments for items delivered, etc. The source of funds, though, is irrelevant to the performance measurement process, except as it constraints the company's ability to perform work, as described above.

Performance budgeting is simply an allocation of the project's total budget, or contract target cost, to the work to be performed in order to give each piece of work a value that is relational to the project's total budget. Theoretically, it should not matter whether the budgets are realistic in terms of being able to actually do the work for that amount. An element of work is only worth so much in terms of total project; and when the work is done, the budget for that work becomes the earned value, regardless of the cost incurred. At the end of the project, the earned value is equal to the project's total authorized budget. So much for theory.

In real life, people want *realistic* budgets to work toward and be measured against. A manager that perceives that the assigned budget is patently unachievable will ignore the budget and manage to some other goal that makes more sense, even if the variance from the official budget must be explained ever month. Thus, it is important that project targets can be as realistic as possible. Otherwise, managers will pay lip service to the project baseline and actually manage to some other informal plan. This is clearly not a desirable situation.

There must be commitment to the original cost and schedule targets (and project scope) by all levels of management at the onset of the project, even if the targets are acknowledged to be very tight. The performance measurement baseline is a reflection of this commitment and represents the plan to achieve those targets. Maintaining a viable baseline in the face of project changes, technical problems, and other challenges can be more difficult and will be discussed later.

CHAPTER 7

Detailed Planning

The performance measurement baseline is established at the control account level, although some far-term work may not be planned to that level at the outset. It should be reiterated that the control account represents a significant amount of work. For major projects, control accounts often average about a year in duration, and it should be possible at the beginning of the project to plan activities to at least that level of detail.

The control account is like a mini-project. It has a defined scope of work, a schedule, a budget, and is interrelated with other control accounts. The control account manager must construct a plan that will ensure the timely accomplishment of the work for the resources that have been allocated. The concepts of work definition, responsibility assignment, scheduling, and budgeting that have been discussed apply also to the control account. The work must be broken into tasks, performing organizations or individuals must be

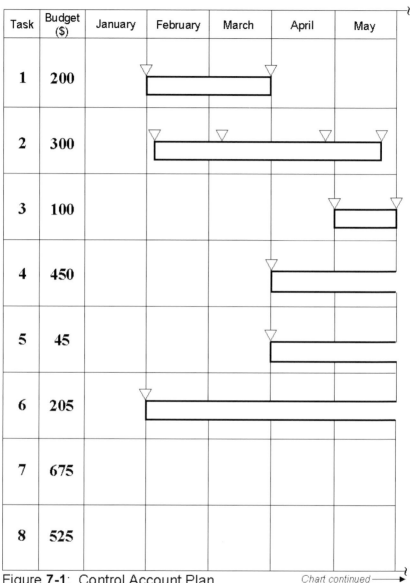

Task	Budget ($)	January	February	March	April	May
1	200					
2	300					
3	100					
4	450					
5	45					
6	205					
7	675					
8	525					

Figure **7-1**: Control Account Plan   *Chart continued* ⟶

identified, and performance targets must be assigned in terms of completion dates and resources available. A control account planning sheet usually serves as the control account manager's master schedule, budget control log, and record

June	July	August	September	October	November	December

← Chart continued

of accomplishments. Figure 7-1 shows a simplified control account plan.

The control account has a designated manager who has the responsibility and authority to plan, schedule, budget, and oversee the accomplishment of the work. Control accounts are subsequently broken into work tasks or lower level jobs, commonly referred to as work packages. The term work package is generic and should not be something new that must be created. Work assignments are normally made via some kind of task assignment sheet or work order (either hard copy or computer screen). These documents have different titles; typical examples are Engineering Task Authorizations, Work Authorization Documents, Shop Orders, Fabrication Orders, Purchase Orders, etc. In most cases, these documents serve also as work package authorizations, because they are used for assigning and controlling the work to be done. A work package could be an engineering drawing or set of drawings. It could be the conduct of a test, the fabrication of a unit, the development of a specification, the writing or testing of a certain number of lines of software code, an analysis study, the assembly of material kits, inspection of items in progress or of completed items, etc. The point is that a work package is simply a defined task or set of tasks that has a completed product or end result. It is a job that can be described, scheduled, budgeted in terms of dollars, labor, or other measurable units, and measured while it is in progress and at its completion.

The concept of short-span work packages often causes concern about the amount of detail and paperwork in the system. But it must be recognized that all work eventually has to be defined, planned, assigned. managed, and reported. Work should not be turned on and off by informal direction and unclear accountability; so the argument that work packaging is too onerous, burdensome, or difficult is not consistent with general good business practices.

In lieu of work packages, some companies use resource-loaded schedules for performance measurement; the idea being to create a detail-level networks and then assign a budget value to each activity on the network. As activities are accomplished, the assigned values are earned and compared to actual costs. This approach goes back to the Department of Defense/NASA concept called PERT-Cost developed during the early 1960's. It is a workable approach but, if care is not exercised, can be more detailed and difficult to maintain than work packages, one of which may cover several activities in a detailed network. Some other problems with this approach are that network activities do not always lend themselves to being costed (many are *dummy* activities), networking is not always the preferred scheduling technique for the type of effort involved, and detail level networks can be difficult and cumbersome for lower level managers to deal with. Problems such as these, in fact, led to the development and incorporation of WBS and work packaging concepts into PERT-Cost; because they were cleaner and simpler to use for work planning, control and measurement. PERT-Cost ultimately was replaced by the Cost/Schedule Control Systems Criteria (C/SCSC) approach, which was a more flexible expression of performance measurement requirements that capitalized on existing systems rather than imposing specific management techniques. The C/SCSC were replaced by the Earned Value Management System Criteria (EVMSC) in 1996. In 1998, the American National Standard Guidelines for Earned Value Management Systems (ANSI/EIA-748-1998) were issued. The term guideline was determined to be less prescriptive than the word criteria. The expected outcome is being realized as more companies begin to adopt Earned Value Management Systems Guidelines (EVMSG).

It should be pointed out that modern computer hardware and software have made the resource-loaded-network approach more viable today than when PERT-Cost was in use, and many of today's project management software packages are based on this approach. However, these software tools also recognize the need for and include the integration of network schedules with work packages and control accounts to provide for effective planning, control, and reporting.

Unfortunately, all work cannot be planned into short-span, discrete work packages. Supporting efforts, such as project management, are not amenable to work packaging, because they take place over protracted periods of time; and activities cannot be scheduled, as there are no final products. These level-of-effort activities usually cannot be measured except through the passage of time, although cost variances can be determined for the resources applied. Level-of-effort should be segregated from measurable activity, either within the control account or in separate control accounts, to avoid distorting the determination of work accomplished that is based on work package completions. Work classified: as level-of-effort should also be kept to a minimum since it is not measuring work accomplished. It only measures the passage of time.

Another kind of activity that must be accommodated is apportioned effort, sometimes called factored effort. Many inspection activities are dealt with on an apportioned basis. For example, a manufacturing work package requires inspection prior to its completion. Rather than create a separate work package, the budget for the inspection activity can be included in the manufacturing work package as a percentage of the overall budget; and that amount can be earned automatically as the work package is accomplished. If desired, a separate work package can be established with its budget as a percentage of the budget for the task to which it is apportioned. As the primary task is accomplished, the value of the apportioned effort task is earned concurrently.

In the event that all work within the control account cannot be planned as work packages, apportioned effort or level-of-effort, larger packages called planning packages may be used. Planning packages are often used to define, to the extent possible, the downstream work in a control account that cannot be planned into work packages at the onset. The primary idea of planning packages is to tie budget and work together as soon as possible. Otherwise, the downstream work might remain undefined and the budget needed for that work could possibly be incorrectly used to deal with current or near-term problems. In addition, key milestones or events which can be identified within planning packages must be included in logic schedules, or no real critical path exists. Figure 7-2 illustrates how a control account can be organized into different kinds of effort.

Task	Budget	January	February	March	April	May
1	**200**		▽⎯⎯⎯⎯⎯⎯⎯⎯▽ Work Package			
2	**300**		▽⎯⎯⎯⎯▽⎯⎯⎯⎯▽⎯⎯⎯⎯▽ Work Package			
3	**100**					▽ Work Package ▽
4	**450**				▽ Work Package	
5	**45**				▽ Apportioned	
6	**205**		▽			Level
7	**675**					
8	**525**					

Figure **7-2**: Control Account Plan   *Chart continued* ⎯⎯→

June	July	August	September	October	November	December
Effort						
Of Effort						
	Planning Package #1					
	Planning Package #2					

Chart continued

CHAPTER 8

Measuring Performance With Earned Value

The key to performance measurement is the objective assessment of work in process. All work is either completed, in-process, or not yet started. Completed work presents no performance measurement problem since those work packages have been closed, the budget has been earned, and progress has been reported. Future work will not be measured until the work gets underway. The only work packages to be concerned about are those that are planned to be or are actually in process at the end of the reporting period, usually the end of the accounting month. Short duration work packages can minimize the work-in-process measurement problem. The longer the work packages, the more difficult it is to determine the actual status of the work and more work packages will be in process at any given point in time.

There is essentially no work-in-process measurement problem associated with a work package that is less than one month in duration and which is planned to be finished before the end of the accounting period. The job is either finished or it isn't. If it is finished, its value is earned. If it is not finished, a schedule variance will occur because the budgeted value for that work will be reported, but that value will not have been earned. In addition, a cost variance will show up if costs have been recorded for the work.

Obviously, all work tasks do not fall out so neatly. Tasks frequently span several reporting periods and may begin and end at various times during the month. In such cases, more sophisticated measurement techniques are necessary. A work package, for example, that spans two reporting periods might employ another technique, such as the 50-50 approach. This technique simply says, plan 50% of the budget when the task is scheduled to start and the other 50% when it is scheduled to be completed; and earn value on that same basis when the job is actually started and is actually completed. This technique will provide both an indication of whether the job started on schedule and whether it was completed on schedule.

For work packages that extend over several months an approach that involves the use of *value milestones* is commonly used. For example, if a work package spans five months in duration, it does not make sense to break it down into two separate work packages. Two or three milestones could be identified within the task to serve as progress indicators, and values, either in terms of individual budgets or percentages of the total work package budget, could be assigned. When a milestone is achieved, the budget associated with that milestone is earned. At least one milestone per reporting period is desirable. However, the milestone events must be clearly defined, objective indicators of physical progress to be effective. In essence, each milestone takes on the characteristics of a work package, but separate work authorization documents are not needed, thus reducing paperwork in the system.

Where a series of units or products is being fabricated, counting completed items and earning the budget associated with each completed unit is a simple approach. An *equivalent unit* technique could also be used. For example, if it takes 100 operations to fabricate an individual unit, and a total of 300 operations have been accomplished, three *equivalent units* have been earned, even though no complete units may have been produced.

These examples could go on ad infinitum, but the important point to be made is that earned value measurement techniques should be adopted that will provide the most objective indicators of work performed. The more they can be based on physical accomplishment, such as completed products, the better. The methods used will vary depending on the types of work involved, time durations, output products, and other factors. The control account manager should determine which technique is most appropriate for each individual work package. Figure 8-1 illustrates a control account plan that employs a variety of planning and measurement techniques.

Measuring performance is relatively straightforward for production and construction activities because there are so many discrete indicators of accomplishment available: units completed, feet of cable pulled, manufacturing operations performed, etc. In large-scale design and engineering development, the problem is more difficult and both detailed

Task	Budget	Earned Value Technique	January	February	March	April
1	200	50-50		100	100	
2	300	Budgeted Milestones		50	75	100
3	100	0-100				
4	450	Units Complete			150 / 3	
5	45	Apportioned Effort			15	
6	205	Level Of Effort		10	20	20
7	675	Planning Package				
8	525	Planning Package				
Control Account Budget = 2500		Month	0	160	195	285
		Cumulative	0	160	355	640

Figure **8-1**: Control Account Plan   *Chart continued* ⟶

planning and performance measurement are harder to accomplish. It is not surprising that engineers want as much

May	June	July	August	September	October	November	December
75							
0 100							
150	150	Units per month at 50 per unit					
3	3						
15	15	Apportioned from task 4 at 10% rate					
30	30	20	20	20	20	10	5
		125	125	125	125	125	50
		100	100	100	100	100	25
370	195	245	245	245	245	235	80
1010	1205	1450	1695	1940	2185	2420	2500

Chart continued

flexibility as possible to permit exploration of different concepts and approaches, thus a requirement to lay out a detailed plan may be resisted. Consequently, a *rolling wave* planning process is often used; i.e., planning the overall effort to a certain level, such as the control account, and progressively planning to the detail level as the work proceeds, trying to stay several months ahead with the detail planning.

Because it is more difficult to get an objective indication of work accomplished for development work, the work package concept takes on more importance. In fact, the original concept of work packaging was advanced as a means of getting a reasonably objective measurement for development activity. Previous measurement techniques were either based on managers' estimates of percent complete or were the result of trying to estimate how much work was left to do. Neither technique worked satisfactorily as most of the time both produced subjective, overstated, optimistic pictures of project performance.

CHAPTER 9

Accounting

In support of project management and performance measurement, the accounting system must be able to relate costs incurred to work accomplished. Most accounting systems were not designed to do this and, if a WBS has not been used, the capability may not exist. Instead, the system may only generate cost of labor, material, and other direct and indirect costs incurred by organizational elements.

The WBS provides a structure that represents the work to be performed, and its integration with the OBS to form control accounts provides a logical place to collect costs.

From the control account, management information, including costs, can be summarized by WBS and by OBS, enabling higher levels of management to look at performance both by element of work and by organization. Significant changes to the accounting system should not be necessary, although a WBS/OBS coding scheme must be adopted to facilitate summarization of data.

Labor charges normally occur at the work package level as labor is electronically input (or recorded on time cards) and accumulated for the control account. Since the control account manager must manage to a budget, labor cost variances should be reviewed both in terms of those variances related to performance (more hours used than planned) and those related to rates (higher cost per hour than planned). Therefore, labor hours should be priced out at the control account level to permit such analysis. In a work-team environment, which involves participants from different functional organizations, labor rates will vary and must be applied within the control account for accurate accounting.

Material costs can be more difficult to deal with for a number of reasons. There are many different kinds of materials, they are purchased and controlled differently, and there are several points in time when material costs can be recorded. For example, at the time a purchase order is placed with a supplier, valuable cost information is available because it is known at the time whether the materials are going to cost more or less than planned. At the time the materials are received, performance of the vendor can be measured. When vendors are paid, the material costs are recorded in the general book of accounts and contractors can bill the customer. Raw materials or miscellaneous items purchased in economic lot quantities may be costed to the project when issued from stores or applied to work in process. In some cases involving production of common parts for various projects, parts are manufactured, put in inventory, and reissued when needed for assembly. The

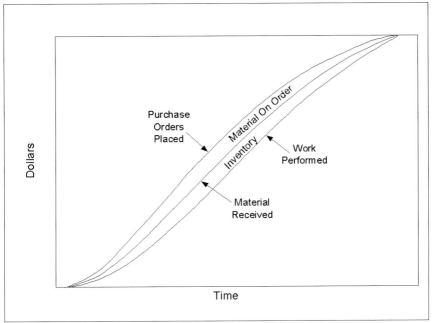

Figure **9-1**:   Material Time Phasing

costs may be allocated as the parts are made or they may be held back until the parts are assigned to a specific project, depending on a variety of factors. Figure 9-1 illustrates the time phasing associated with the material acquisition process.

As with labor, material costs should also be analyzed in terms of two components: price variance (materials cost more than planned) and usage variance (more materials used than planned). The price variance can be determined when the purchase order is placed. The usage variance is determined when the work is being done.

A performance measurement system is intended to reveal whether work performed is costing more or less than it was planned to cost. Based on that premise, it would seem to make sense that material costs, like labor, should be recorded only when the work is performed. This approach, however, *delays* the visibility of material cost problems. As previously noted, the portion of the material cost problem related to price is available at the time the purchase order is placed. Material price variances should be surfaced and incorporated into project cost estimates at that time, even though the actual costs are still a long way from entering the books of account.

A rational approach that accommodates performance measurement considerations is to record the costs of most materials at the time the materials are received. Material deliveries do represent progress of work and earned value can logically be taken at that time. However, the actual costs used for performance measurement would have to be estimated actuals, based on purchase order, invoice, or other information, since the actual costs will not enter the formal books until the suppliers are paid. If necessary, an accounting adjustment can be made to ensure compatibility with the book of accounts after payment. Raw materials could continue to be costed and their value earned when they are issued to work in process.

Material costs can be recorded by work package, but it is more common to charge those costs directly to the control account. Other direct costs, such as travel costs, may also be charged directly to the control account. Eventually, labor, material, and other direct costs must be expressed in dollars, and all elements can be converted to dollars at the control account level, whereas labor may only be recorded only in terms of hours at the work package level.

Major subcontractors may receive a flow down of performance requirements, and their reports must be integrated into the prime contractor's system and reports. Large subcontracts can be treated as separate WBS elements; others may be integrated with the WBS at the control account level. One problem that must be dealt with, though, is the lag time associated with subcontractor reporting. It may not be possible to align the accounting period cut-off dates so as to incorporate subcontract reporting in the current month. Consequently, users of the cost performance reports must understand that the bottom line may not represent the total project as of the reporting cut-off date. This should not be a big problem unless the subcontractor is experiencing significant difficulties. In these cases, a "flash" report from the subcontractor may be in order and the prime contractor should highlight the problem in the narrative portion of the project performance report. Electronic data interchange can also improve the timeliness of subcontractor reporting.

Supplies that get progress payments based on costs incurred and evidence of physical accomplishment must also be represented in the baseline plan. Budgets can be based on the progress payment plan with earned value (Budgeted Cost for Work Preformed) and actual costs (Actual Costs of Work Performed) based on milestone accomplishments and actual payments made. Unlike prime contractor cost reporting, subcontractor costs include fee or profit, as applicable, which represents cost to the prime.

The WBS/OBS integration and cost element delineation within the control account provides a structure that allows detailed visibility of cost information. Figure 9-2 illustrates how the engineering direct labor costs for specific WBS element can be easily identified within the system.

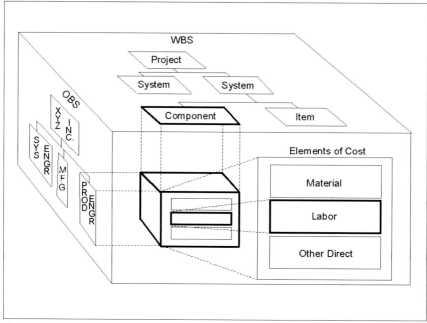

Figure **9-2**: WBS/OBS/Cost Element Identification

Indirect costs are normally collected in overhead pools at a summary organizational level and then allocated back to projects and contracts using rates that are based on a ratio of direct to indirect costs. Indirect cost impacts may or may not be visible to the control account manager, depending on individual company practices.

CHAPTER 10

Data Collection

All of the data elements needed for performance measurement come together in the control account. The control account manager analyzes data, trends, and variances, and takes appropriate corrective actions. The principal data elements that reflect performance are budget, (or BCWS), earned value, (or BCWP) and actual cost (or ACWP). Earned value is the key element because it represents progress of work. When earned value is compared to the budget for that work, a *schedule variance* is derived. When it is compared to the actual costs incurred, a *cost variance* is derived. To be comparable, all three data elements must relate to the same work and the same time period.

The control account planning sheet can be used to reflect ongoing performance based on work package accomplishments. The first meaningful variance analysis takes place at

Control Account	Budget	Earned Value Technique	January	February	March	April
1	200	50-50		100	100	
2	300	Budgeted Milestones		50	75	100
3	100	0-100				
4	450	Units Complete				150 / 3
5	45	Apportioned Effort				15
6	205	Level Of Effort	10	20	20	
7	675	Planning Package				
8	525	Planning Package				

Control Account Status		January	February	March	April
	Mo Budget	0	160	195	285
	Cum Budget	0	160	355	640
	Mo Earned Value	0	160	195	285
	Cum Earned Value	0	160	355	640
	Mo Actual Cost	0	125	210	379
	Cum Actual Cost	0	125	335	714

Figure **10-1**: Control Account Status   *Chart continued* ➝

the control account level for several reasons: (1) material cost information may not be available at the work package level, (2) earned value is determined at the control account level by accumulating the budgeted values for completed work package and the work-in-process, (3) the control account contains a large enough aggregation of work to

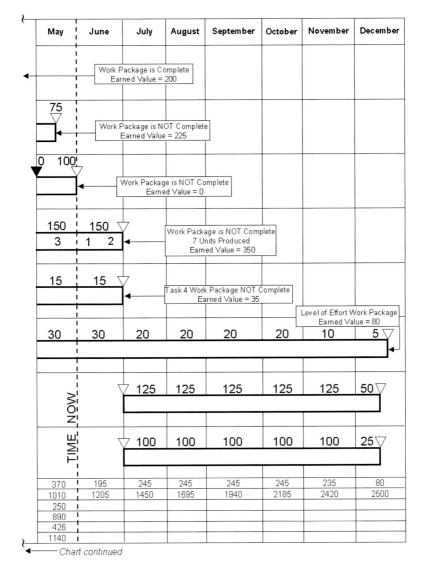

May	June	July	August	September	October	November	December

Work Package is Complete
Earned Value = 200

75

Work Package is NOT Complete
Earned Value = 225

0 100

Work Package is NOT Complete
Earned Value = 0

| 150 | 150 | | | | | | |
| 3 | 1 | 2 | | | | | |

Work Package is NOT Complete
7 Units Produced
Earned Value = 350

| 15 | 15 | | | | | | |

Task 4 Work Package NOT Complete
Earned Value = 35

Level of Effort Work Package
Earned Value = 80

| 30 | 30 | 20 | 20 | 20 | 20 | 10 | 5 |

TIME NOW

| | | 125 | 125 | 125 | 125 | 125 | 50 |

| | | 100 | 100 | 100 | 100 | 100 | 25 |

370	195	245	245	245	245	235	80
1010	1205	1450	1695	1940	2185	2420	2500
250							
890							
426							
1140							

Chart continued

make variance analysis meaningful, and (4) the control account manager is responsible for getting the work done and reporting to the project manager. Using the control account plan shown in Figure 8-1, a control account status report is illustrated in Figure 10-1.

The control account shown has eight work packages.

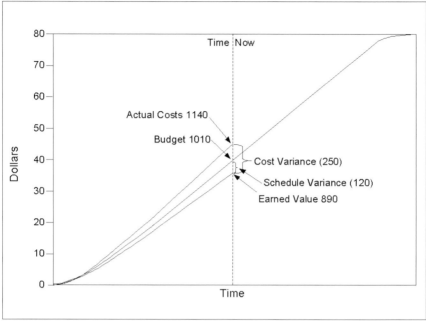

Figure **10-2**: Cumulative Performance

Three work packages were planned to have been completed and three others partially completed for an accumulated budget of 1010. One of the work packages has been accomplished for an earned value of 200. The other five have begun but only partially complete, earning a value of 690 for a total of 890. Actual costs recorded against the control account are 1140. Therefore, the work is behind schedule and over cost. The value of the work that did not get done (schedule variance) is -120 (earned value of 890 minus budget of 1010) and the cost variance is -250 (earned value of 890 minus actual costs of 1140). Figure 10-2 portrays the data graphically in terms of cumulative performance.

These data can be combined with other control accounts to show the status of any WBS or OBS element. Performance

WBS	Current Period (May)					Cumulative To Date				
	Budget	Earned Value	Actual Costs	Variance		Budget	Earned Value	Actual Costs	Variance	
				Schedule	Cost				Schedule	Cost
CA1	370	250	426	(120)	(176)	1010	890	1140	(120)	(250)
CA2	8	7	8	(1)	(1)	40	38	42	(2)	(4)
CA3	7	7	8	0	(1)	13	12	12	(1)	0
CA4	10	6	12	(4)	(6)	46	40	51	(6)	(11)
CA5	12	10	13	(2)	(3)	12	10	13	(2)	(3)
Total	407	280	467	(127)	(187)	1121	990	1258	(131)	(268)

Figure **10-3**: Performance Report

can be reported for the last reporting period (month) or cumulative-to-date. A typical reporting format is shown in figure 10-3.

In this example, five control accounts make up the WBS element being reported. The bottom line shows the overall status, which is behind schedule (131) and overrunning cost (268). The cumulative cost and schedule variance columns indicate the control accounts that are encountering the most problems. Control accounts #1 and #4 are having significant cost and schedule problems. The current period cost and schedule variances indicate that performance deteriorated considerably during the month.

WBS element data can be summarized to any level desired for management reporting, although WBS level

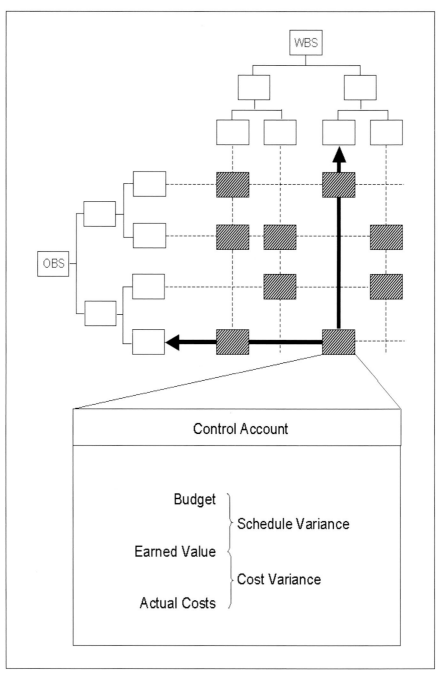

Figure **10-4**: Summarization of Data

Budget	Earned Value	Actual Cost	INTERPRETATION
100	100	100	On schedule, on cost
100	120	120	Ahead of schedule, on cost
120	100	100	Behind schedule, on cost
100	100	120	On schedule, over cost
100	120	140	Ahead of schedule, over cost
120	100	120	Behind schedule, over cost
120	120	100	On schedule, under cost
100	120	100	Ahead of schedule, under cost
140	120	100	Behind schedule, under cost

Figure **10-5**: Interpretation of Data

three is normally used. The same kind of information can also be accumulated through the OBS to obtain performance of individual organizations. Figure 10-4 illustrates this dual summarization capability.

An important point is that all calculations are made at the control account level by the manager responsible for getting the work done. Performance calculations at higher levels are not necessary, and variances can be easily traced from summary reports back to the responsible control accounts through either the WBS or the OBS.

Nine different combinations of project status can be elicited from these data elements as shown in Figure 10-5.

CHAPTER 11

Estimating Cost At Completion

"The Sabanes-Oxley Act of 2002 is forcing many companies to adopt significant changes to their internal controls and the roles played by their audit committees and senior management in the financial reporting process. Consequently, the Estimated Cost at Completion (EAC), an important forecast in the financial report, is now a very key, signatory Project Cost Estimate." *Gary C. Humphreys, The 14th Annual International Integrated project Management Conference, November, 2002.*

Cost estimating is often called a black art and, too often, estimates are structured to fit some predetermined idea of a number that is politically salable. When ranges of estimates are prepared, opponents of the project tend to focus on the high end while proponents want to look at the low end. In the final analysis, most cost estimates are products of man-

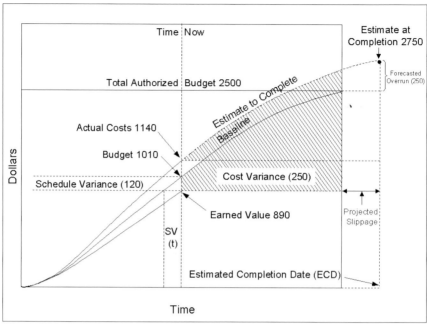

Figure **11-1**: Estimate Based on Baseline Achievement

agement judgement. They are affected by political considerations, budgetary considerations, important upcoming
events, such as technical reviews, and other factors. There is
also the feeling that more/better information will be available next month or next quarter, so perhaps the estimate
update should wait until then.

Advocates of performance measurement have been
accused of concentrating too much on historical information
while the project manager, company management, and the
customer are more interested in what lies ahead and what
the final cost will be. However, to figure out what the cost
will be at completion requires an evaluation of the work
remaining, and to determine how much work is remaining
requires a solid understanding of where the project is now.

Performance measurement provides that essential information because earned value represents the amount of work accomplished in terms of the overall project target. Subtracting earned value from the total authorized budget reveals the budgeted cost for the work remaining, (BCWR).

All estimating is based on assumptions. If the assumption is that this project is just like the last project, historical data provides the estimate. If it is similar, but more complex, a "complexity factor" can be applied to make the estimate more realistic.

The performance measurement baseline represents the plan for doing the project, and considerable effort is expended to make it a meaningful, workable plan. It is updated as the project moves along to incorporate changes in scope or direction, and revised to compensate for problems experienced along the way. Assuming that the baseline validity is maintained, a very simplified estimate of cost at completion can be derived by simply adding the cumulative cost variance to the total authorized budget. Figure 11-1 illustrates this approach.

Target cost (2500) minus earned value (890) equals the budget for work remaining (1610). Actual costs (1140) plus the budget for work remaining (1610) equals the estimate at completion (2750). Since the current cost variance is -250, if the plan for the remaining work is achieved, and the cost variance does not change when added to the total authorized budget, it provides an estimate at completion of 2750; total authorized budget (2500) plus the cost variance (-250).

If, however, the project has been overrunning, using the baseline plan from now to completion represents *improved performance*, and an explanation should be provided as to

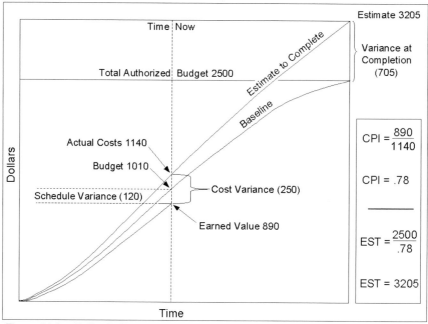

Figure **11-2**: Estimate Based on Continuance of Actual Performance

how this improvement will be achieved. Studies of hundreds of projects have revealed that project performance does *not* tend to improve. In fact, once the project passes the 15% completion point, performance almost never surpasses the average performance to date, and often gets worse. Average performance to date can be easily calculated by dividing the cumulative earned value by the cumulative actual costs. The resultant value is called the Cost Performance Index (CPI), and a number less than 1 reflects unfavorable cost performance. For example, a CPI of 0.85 means that for every dollar being spent, only 85 cents worth of work has been done. Dividing the total project budget by the CPI of 0.85 will provide a cost estimate that reflects a continuation of performance to date to the end of the project.

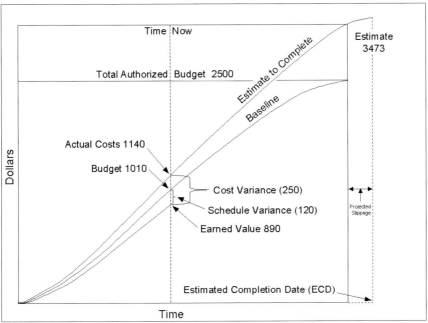

Figure **11-3**: Estimate Based on Combined Cost and Schedule Performance

Project managers, in reports to senior management, should be asked to explain any estimate lower than that derived using the CPI approach. Figure 11-2 illustrates the CPI technique where the earned value (890) is divided by the actual costs (1140) to produce a CPI (0.78). Dividing the total project budget (2500) by the CPI (0.78) results in an estimate for the project of 3205. This approach is simply a linear extrapolation and does not take schedule projections into consideration. In essence, it assumes that if the project is 10% overrun today, it will be 10% overrun at completion. If desired, A CPI can be calculated for a recent period of performance (e.g., last 6 months) if there is reason to believe it would produce a higher quality estimate.

If dividing earned value by actual costs provides a cost

performance index, then dividing earned value (890) by the cumulative budget (1010) provides a schedule performance index (SPI) of 0.88. If the project is not only overrunning cost, but is also behind schedule, additional cost impact can be expected either because of potential schedule slippage or from acceleration of the effort to finish on time; both alternatives cost money. Multiplying the CPI (0.78) by the SPI (0.88) provides a composite index (0.69) that can be applied to the budget for work remaining (1610 divided by 0.69 equals 2333) and added to the actual costs (1140) to produce yet another estimate (3473). Figure 11-3 illustrates this concept.

Thus a range of estimates (2750, 3205, 3473) can be derived quickly and easily from the performance measurement data elements of budget, earned value and actual costs. These estimates should not be used as the final cost estimates, but as a sanity check for the cost estimates derived through other methods, such as engineering estimates, grass roots estimates, parametric estimates, other statistical estimates, and estimates based on management experience.

At least annually, the contractor should perform a comprehensive estimate of cost at completion using a variety of estimating techniques. This estimate is needed in support of business based projections, the annual financial plan, baseline revisions, and cash flow management. The statistical techniques described above are used to update the estimate as time passes and as a cross-check against unrealistic projections.

CHAPTER 12

Change Control

Rarely, if ever, does a project proceed without changes, which is unfortunate because changes are disruptive and expensive. Poorly planned and executed projects are much more susceptible to change activity than are those that are well thought out prior to initiating the work. Regardless, changes are a fact of life and must be accommodated.

Changes generally fall into two categories; externally directed changes and internal replanning. External changes usually involve changes in scope, schedule, or funding. Internal replanning is intended to compensate for problems being experienced, to achieve efficiencies in operation, or to change work plans.

External changes are those directed by management or resulting from contract modifications. Such changes should be incorporated into work plans as quickly as possible to

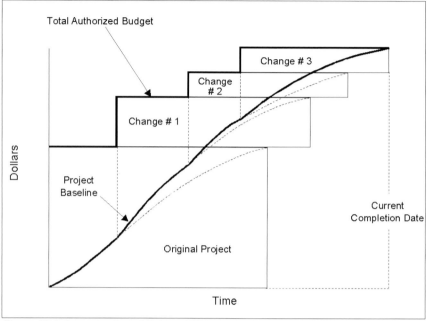

Figure **12-1**: Incorporation of External Changes

ensure that the project baseline remains current. Failure to do so on a dynamic project can cause changes to accumulate and force people to work to informal plans because of the administrative delays in updating baseline documentation. External changes usually result in an increase in the total project budget, extension of the project schedule, or a combination of the two. Figure 12-1 illustrates the effects of such changes on the project baseline.

Externally directed changes are not always generated by company management or by the customer. Many changes are initiated through engineering change proposals and other ideas offered by company employees as ways to improve the product. These proposals are normally evaluated and endorsed by a change control board before being submitted to management or to the customer. Formal authorization is required before changes are incorporated into the project, including the establishment of cost, schedule, and technical targets for the new scope of work. A change control log should be maintained to show how the original project has evolved over time. Figure 12-2 is an example of a baseline control log.

The WBS dictionary, control account planning sheets, and other pertinent documentation should be updated to reflect changes as appropriate. In the event of post-contract claims or liability disputes, these updated records become invaluable in determining effects of actions taken and responsibility for them.

Unlike external changes, which usually affect cost and schedule targets, internal replanning only changes the shape of the baseline curve because of shifts of work elements or changes to schedules and budgets. Internal changes usually are necessitated by technical problems. Test failures, performance shortfalls, design deficiencies, manufacturing problems, and other technical difficulties require additional resources in terms of budget and schedule. Additional budget comes from management reserve, from work deletions, or from other work if efficiencies can be found that will free up resources. Figure 12-3 illustrates the effects on the baseline resulting from internal replanning using management reserve.

When management reserve budget is used, it is transferred from the reserve log into control accounts. Transfers of management reserve are tracked and reported because they are often problem indicators. When work is moved from one time period to another, or from one organization to

Date	Change	Contract Target Cost	Authorized Unpriced Work	Total Authorized Budget
1/02	ABC Contract	120	-	120
1/25	Contract Chg 001	20	-	20
1/31	January Summary	140	-	140
2/5	Change 002	-	45	45
2/15	Change 003	-	30	30
2/23	Contract Chg 004	30	-	30
2/28	February Summary	170	75	245
3/6	Changes 002 and 003 negotiated	70	-	(5)
3/31	March Summary	240	-	240

Figure **12-2**: Baseline Control Log

Chart continued ⟶

Manage-ment Reserve	PM Baseline	Undistri-buted Budget	Direct Budget	O/H Budget	G & A Budget
10	110	10	40	40	20
2	18	-	8	8	2
12	128	10	48	48	22
0	45	20	11	11	3
0	30	19	5	5	1
2	28	-	12	12	4
14	231	49	76	76	30
3	(8)	(39)	14	14	3
17	223	10	90	90	33

← *Chart continued*

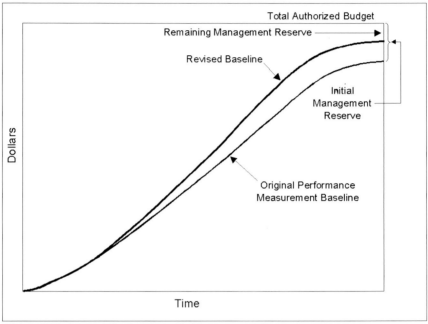

Figure **12-3**: Internal Replanning with Management Reserve

another, the budget assigned to that work should go with it. Keeping work and budget tied together is an important concept that normally would not be violated in a performance measurement system, although a major replanning may result in a redistribution of resources. In such cases, management and the customer must be kept informed of baseline changes and their rationale.

Replanning of future work plans can occur at any time, and it is important that changes be controlled and understood. Overlaying a plot of the current baseline on top of the

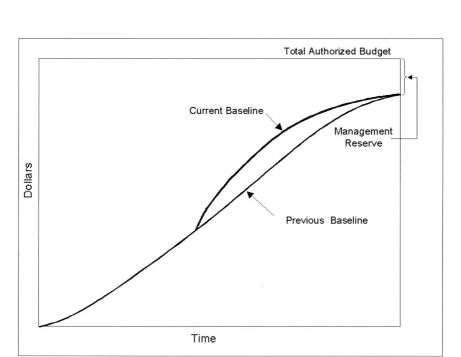

Figure **12-4**: Internal Replanning-Rephasing Work or Budget

previous month's baseline may reveal inappropriate shifts of work or budget. Figure 12-4 indicates that downstream work or budget has been moved forward in time. If only budget has been moved, it is important to identify the work from which it was taken. Otherwise, a significant downstream surprise may await.

CHAPTER 13

Baseline Maintenance

Maintaining the baseline throughout the project is probably the most difficult aspect of the performance measurement process. External changes to project scope must be accommodated so that the baseline accurately represents the current project. Timely incorporation of changes is necessary so that managers are not tracking to obsolete plans and generating false variances. A systematic process should be established for updating the baseline with a minimum amount of disruption to work in process.

Accommodating internal replanning actions can also present problems, particularly if the management reserve budget is nearly gone. The performance measurement system must have sufficient flexibility to permit managers to deal with problems, but not be so loose that problems are not surfaced in a timely manner. For example, if a manager is able to continually add budget to tasks that are in trouble, cost variances will not occur until all budget has been exhausted with work remaining to be done. This has the effect of *bow-waving* problems downstream and reducing or eliminating options for cost recovery. Thus, a certain amount of baseline discipline is required to make the system function effectively.

Baseline discipline falls somewhere between two extremes: maintaining a rigid baseline that cannot be changed except for external changes, and allowing the baseline to change whenever variances are imminent. The project manager must establish appropriate groundrules for internal replanning.

Each control account eventually receives a budget and schedule within which the work is planned to be accomplished, and the control account manager should have the flexibility to replan future work within those constraints. In very long control accounts, planning packages can be used to ensure that sufficient budget is reserved for downstream work.

If work proceeds according to plan, the performance measurement process is very straight forward and variances from the plan reflect minor perturbations associated with work performance. However, if problems develop, additional resources may be needed to accommodate rework or new tasks. If the control account manager cannot work the problem within the overall control account budget, only two options are available: do the work and (1) show the resulting cost variance, or (2) request additional budget from the management reserve. The project manager must decide whether to use management reserve for this particular problem. Consequently, the cost problem will be reflected as either an unfavorable cost variance or as use of management reserve or both.

If no management reserve is available, the problem for the control account manager becomes more difficult. Since budgets are being used for measuring performance, the concept of "zero-budget work packages" is not popular among those who must do the work. To solve this problem, some companies authorize operating budgets to provide internal targets for work that cannot be accommodated within the total authorized budget. Operating budgets can be used to track performance within the control account but do not become part of the reported earned value because the control account budget must maintain its relationship to the total authorized budget. Therefore, the control account manager must either keep operating budgets separate from project budgets, or delete the operating budget before reporting earned value to higher management. One approach for doing this involves factoring out the operating budget at the control account level. For example, a control account budget is set at 100. At some point it becomes obvious that the work is going to cost 120. No management reserve is available, but use of an operating budget is authorized. An additional budget of 20 is authorized to the remaining work packages. At the end of the reporting period, budget and earned value are collected based on the total budget of 120. Before reporting control account status to higher levels, the control account manager eliminates the operating budget by multiplying the budget and earned value by a factor of 0.833, (100 divided by 120). This calculation reduces the budget and earned value to reflect cost performance in terms of the total authorized budget. Actual costs are not affected. If desired by the project manager, the control account manager can also report performance in

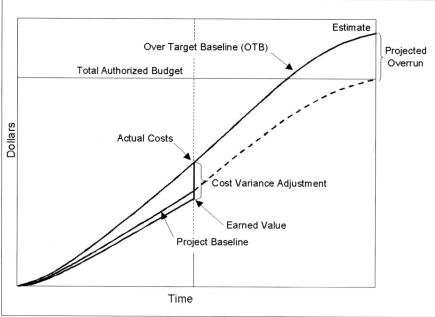

Figure **13-1**: The Over Target Baseline (Cost and Schedule Variances Eliminated)

terms of the operating budget in a separate report.

Use of the operating budget concept should be limited to specific problem areas. If the project is in such severe difficulty that virtually everybody needs budgetary relief, a revision to the total authorized budget is probably in order. For internal company projects, this is a senior-level management decision to revise the project goals. In a contractual situation, the problem is more difficult. Contract target costs cannot be changed unilaterally, and the customer may not be inclined or able to change the total authorized budget for a variety of reasons. It may, however, be possible to reach agreement with the customer to measure performance to a goal other than the total authorized budget. The new goal, called an overtarget baseline, would be established for man-

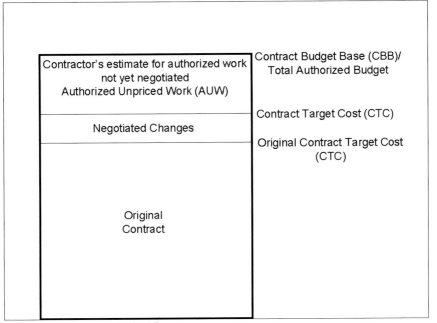

Figure **13-2**: Contract Budget Base

agement purposes and would not effect the contractual arrangements. Figure 13-1 illustrates one version of the overtarget baseline.

Adopting an overtarget baseline should not be taken lightly since it essentially represents a formal declaration of an overrun, builds the overrun into the baseline plan, distorts performance measurement on the project to some degree, and complicates reporting. However, it is a way to deal with performance measurement on projects that are experiencing major cost problems. Without such an alternative, performance measurement system disciplines tend to break down, because the baseline may no longer be representative of the work that is being done.

Until this point, the baseline discussion has been oriented

to total authorized budgets or contract budget base. On some contracts, the negotiated contract target cost (or estimated cost in the case of cost-plus contracts) may not represent the total contract value. Occasionally, contractors are authorized to perform work *before* costs are negotiated. In such cases, the Contract Baseline consists of the sum of the negotiated costs *plus* the contractor's estimate for authorized work that has not yet been negotiated. This amount is referred to as the Contract Budget Base. The sum of the distributed budgets, undistributed budgets, and management reserve should always equal the Contract Budget Base unless an overtarget baseline has been authorized. Figure 13-2 illustrates the elements of the Contract budget Base.

CHAPTER 14

External Reporting

Performance data collected at the control account level can be summarized for progressively higher levels of the WBS and the OBS to provide project status to management and to the customer. Care must be taken in selecting the appropriate WBS level of summarization to avoid unnecessary detail. Typically, a WBS expands at a rate of about six elements per level of indenture. This means that level two would consist of six elements, level three about thirty-six elements, level four about 200 elements, and so on. WBS level three is usually selected as the best level for overall reporting with, perhaps, a few elements of special interest reported at level four. Some support elements may be reported only at level two. It should be no problem for the computer to organize the data for the desired level. Reporting on 20 to 30 WBS elements will provide plenty of visibility into project cost/schedule performance. More detail can be obtained on an exception basis for those WBS elements that are experiencing significant variances.

Organizational performance measurement is usually reported at level two, which would constitute the major internal organizations and significant subcontracts. In a contractual situation, the customer is more interested in the WBS orientation because it represents the products or services being purchased, while the contractor wants to look also at organizational performance.

Since the data being reported simply rolls up from the control account, there is usually no need for higher level calculations with one exception – the estimate of cost at completion. Control account managers' estimates will be reviewed, and possibly adjusted, by managers at higher levels, since a straight accumulation of lower level estimates sometimes results in unrealistically high numbers at the summary level if they are not tempered by management experience and a broader view of the project.

The main concern with selecting appropriate levels of detail for reporting is the amount of variance analysis required and time spent explaining and documenting variances. It is important that reasonable thresholds or groundrules defining significant variances be established to avoid administrative costs and excessive documentation and explanations. A typical performance report is depicted in Figure 14-1.

A single performance report is essentially a snapshot of project status at a point in time. The report in Figure 14-1 reveals the following information at a glance:

- the Total line indicates that the project is ahead of schedule – more work was done (285) than was planned (277).
- the project is overrunning cost – earned value (285) is less than actual cost (292).

- the project is forecast to be underrun at completion – budget (594) versus estimate (573).
- the cost variance column reveals that WBS element 3.2 is experiencing the largest cost problem – cumulative cost variance (-8).
- WBS element 3.2 is forecasting an improving trend in cost *performance* in the future – at completion variance (-12) versus cumulative cost variance (-8) with less than half the work done. The current rate of cost performance is 0.88 – earned value (60) divided by actual cost (68) equals CPI (0.88). Dividing the total budget (160) by the CPI (0.88) indicates an estimate at completion of 182 for this WBS element. An explanation for the estimate reported (172) should be requested, as the to-complete cost performance with the 172 EAC is .96 or a .08 improvement.
- Performance against the performance measurement baseline indicates an overrun (-4) while the Total line indicates an underrun (21). The difference is the availability of management reserve (25). In this example, the project manager is not forecasting the use of any management reserve; thus offsetting the unfavorable cost variance (-4) and underrunning the project by 21. If, on the other hand, the project manager believes that all the management reserve will be gone by the end of the project, 25 would be entered in the estimate at completion column and an overrun of 4 would show on the Total line. The project manager should enter in the estimate column the amount of management reserve expected to be used (based on risk analysis, experience, quality of estimates, etc.) to reflect the most realistic projection possible on the bottom line.

WBS Elements	CUMULATIVE		
	Budget	Earned Value	Actual Costs
Item 3.1	35	39	40
Item 3.2	62	60	68
Item 3.3	14	13	14
Item 3.4	125	127	120
Item 3.5	41	46	50
Undistributed Budget			
PM Baseline	277	285	292
Management Reserve			
Total	277	285	292

Figure **14-1**: Performance Report

Chart continued ➝

TO DATE		AT COMPLETION		
Schedule Variance	Cost Variance	Budget	Estimate	Variance
4	(1)	95	95	0
(2)	(8)	160	172	(12)
(1)	(1)	72	72	0
2	7	165	155	10
5	(4)	63	65	(2)
		14	14	0
8	(7)	569	573	(4)
		25	0	25
8	(7)	594	573	21

Chart continued

PERFORMANCE MEASUREMENT BASE-						
Budget cum to date	Budget for report period	Budget for months				
		+1	+2	+3	+4	+5

CHANGES TO BASELINE	
Change No.	Descrip-

PERFORMANCE MEASUREMENT BASE-						
Budget cum to date	Budget for months					
	+1	+2	+3	+4	+5	+6

Figure **14-2**: Baseline Report *Chart continued* ⟶

Another report worth considering is a baseline report. Such a report is shown in Figure 14-2.

LINE – BEGINNING OF REPORT PERIOD

	Quarters		Years		Undist Budget	Total
	+1	+2	+1	+2		

DURING REPORT PERIOD

tion	Budget

LINE – END OF REPORT PERIOD

	Quarters		Years		Undist Budget	Total
	+1	+2	+1	+2		
Chart continued			Management Reserve			
			Total Budget			

This report reflects how the budget has been time phased by month for 6 months, then by other time periods, such as quarters or years, out to the end of the project. Changes that occur during the reporting period are listed with their associated budgets. The bottom line shows the net adjustment to the baseline as a result of change incorporation. The data on this line will move up to the top line on the next report. The information can be plotted to visually display the effects of baseline changes on the shape of the curve. The rubber baseline problem can be discerned by comparing successive plots of the performance measurement baseline.

The schedule variance reported on the performance report is only an indicator of schedule conditions. It is not intended to be a substitute for the scheduling system and the reports that emanate therefrom. Schedule reporting will vary from project to project depending on the scheduling system and software being used. The reports should provide a schedule baseline and clearly indicate progress against that plan. They should also show the impacts of problems on the project end date and on key project milestones. Schedule reporting must be integrated with technical performance measurement to insure that milestones are not reported complete until all technical requirements have been satisfied.

CHAPTER 15

Graphic Presentation Of Data

A single performance report provides the status of the project at a point in time. When combined with previous reports, a much more revealing picture of the project emerges since performance trends become visible. Trend information is useful, because trends tend to continue and can be very hard to reverse. A popular depiction of project performance is shown in Figure 15-1.

Although the chart seems complicated at first glance, it provides a clear picture of what has happed to the project since its inception. The solid stairstep line shows the increases to the project baseline. The dashed line shows the changes to the estimated cost at completion. The estimated completion date reflects extensions to the original planned completion date. The cumulative budget line represents the performance measurement baseline with the difference between the end of that line and the total authorized budget/contract budget base indicating remaining management reserve. The earned value reflects progress of work achieved

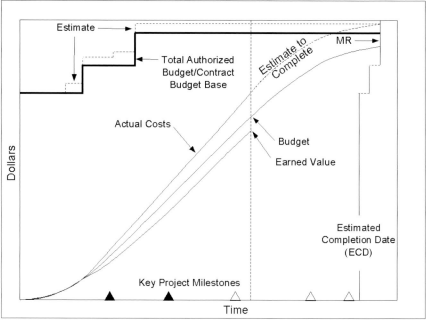

Figure **15-1**: Cumulative Performance

and, when compared to actual costs, shows the cost variance on the project. The milestones help to put project status in perspective. The chart shows a project that is about 60% complete, is behind schedule, and overrunning costs, and performance is getting progressively worse. There have been two changes to the total authorized budget/contract budget base and two schedule extensions, and a key milestone has not been completed as planned.

A second chart provides additional insight into cost and schedule performance trends as shown in Figure 15-2.

In this presentation, the horizontal center line represents earned value since both the schedule and cost variance are derived by subtracting the budget and actual costs from the earned value. Data plotted below the line reflects unfavor-

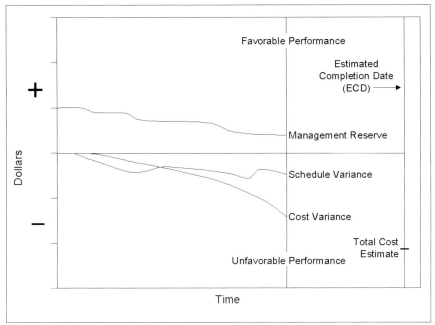

Figure **15-2**: Cost and Schedule Variance Trends

able performance. This example indicates that the project fell behind schedule early and is incurring significant unfavorable cost variances. The schedule variance trend line reflects the effect often caused by baseline replanning. Typically, when the baseline is adjusted, behind-schedule work gets rescheduled into the future. When this is done, the budget is set equal to the earned value, which eliminates the schedule variance. Resetting to earned value is done because replanning takes place from where the project really is, which is represented by the earned value, not from where it was planned to be, which is represented by the budget. The cost variance trend is not affected, since earned value and actual costs are not changed.

Management reserve usage is also plotted on this chart,

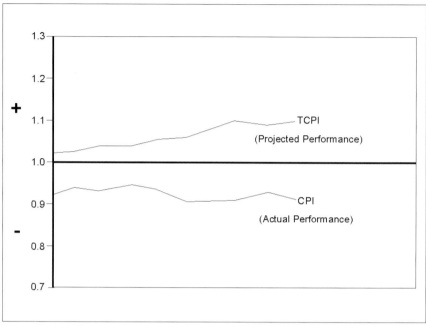

Figure **15-3**: Actual vs. Projected Performance

since use of management reserve tends to dampen out the cost variance. This happens because the application of reserve budget increases the value of the work to which it is applied, thus avoiding a cost variance that would otherwise appear.

Numerous problem indicators are revealed by these charts. Usually the first bad sign is an unfavorable schedule variance, which indicates that planned work is not getting done. Even though there may not be a cost variance at this point, deviating from plan almost certainly will have an unfavorable cost impact, since it costs money to catch up and it costs money to stretch things out.

The second problem indicator is often the application of management reserve to compensate for the deviation from plan. An unfavorable cost variance will appear if problems persist. Baseline replanning may soon follow. This cycle tends to repeat during the life of the project.

Another problem indicator may be the rate at which actual costs are being incurred. If the baseline is front loaded, cost variances may not appear until the project is well along. Once a level of resources (workforce) is dedicated to a project, costs will accrue at a very predictable rate until the workforce level is reduced. The key milestones plotted in Figure 15-1 will help to identify when significant workforce changes are feasible. Up to that point, the actual cost line will be virtually a straight line, and a projection of that line should not be ignored.

A way to evaluate the credibility of the estimate at completion is depicted in Figure 15-3.

This chart compares the cost performance index (CPI) (earned value divided by actual costs) to the to-complete performance index (TCPI) (budget for work remaining divided by the estimated cost for work remaining). The chart shows a CPI of 0.9, which means that for every dollar being spent only 90 cents worth of the work is getting done. The TCPI of 1.1 means that $1.10 worth of work must be done for every dollar spent to meet the current estimate at completion. Clearly, the estimate is not based on performance to date. Any gap between the CPI and the TCPI means that future performance is projected to be different than actual performance being experienced.

There are many other ways to organize and display the standard performance measurement data elements, but these three charts provide considerable visibility into project performance. These kind of charts can be prepared for individual WBS or OBS elements (as well as for the total project) where such detail is warranted. Several automated programs exist that perform all the required calculations, produce these and other graphics, and calculate statistical estimates at completion based on various performance factors.

C H A P T E R

EVMSG

16

In December 1996, the Department of Defense replaced the nearly three decades old Cost/Schedule Control Systems Criteria (C/SCSC) with the updated Earned Value Management Systems Criteria (EVMSC), now called Earned Value Management Systems Guidelines (EVMSG), for evaluating the quality of management systems used on major system acquisition contracts. These guidelines have also been adopted by many other U.S. government agencies and by government agencies within the countries of Australia and Canada. Data emanating from systems that comply with the EVMSG have been proven to provide objective reports of contract status, numerous indicators of actual or impending cost problems, and significant information for projecting future contract cost performance on major contracts.

The EVMSG consist of 32 criteria organized into 5 basic categories: Organization, Planning and Budgeting, Accounting Considerations, Analysis and Management Reports, and Revisions and Data Maintenance. In general terms, the guidelines require contractors to define the contractual scope of work using a WBS; identify organizational responsibility for the work; integrate internal management subsystems; authorize, schedule and budget the work; measure progress of work based on objective indicators; collect costs of labor and material associated with work performed; analyze variances from planned costs and schedules; forecast cost at contract completion; and control changes.

Government teams through a systematic review process called a Compliance Evaluation determine contractor compliance with the guidelines. The contractor will demonstrate how the EVMS is structured and used in actual operation. Compliance is recognized by issuing a Letter of Acceptance, which the contractor may use in response to future solicitations requiring EVMSG. After the initial acceptance of a contractor's EVMS, no further system evaluation reviews will be conducted unless there is a serious need determined by the government. A shorter review normally conducted early in the program, called an Integrated Baseline Review, is undertaken to substantiate the validity of the performance measurement baseline.

The guideline approach gives contractors considerable flexibility in selecting management approaches. In fact, the contractor can use virtually any system or technique as long as it possesses the capabilities and disciplines required by the guidelines. Although they are more explicitly stated, EMVSC and the industry standard, the EVMS guidelines, ANSI/EIA-748-1998, are consistent with the performance measurement concepts expressed in earlier chapters of this book. The following sections paraphrase the individual criteria in basic terms.

Organization

1. Define all contract work using a WBS.
2. Identify the organizations that will do the work.
3. Integrate internal management subsystems with each other and the WBS.
4. Identify the managers of overhead costs.
5. Measure cost and schedule performance by WBS and organization elements.

Planning and Budgeting

1. Schedule the work to meet contractual requirements.
2. Identify products and indicators of output.
3. Establish a budget baseline based on the negotiated contract cost.
4. Segregate budgets in terms of labor, material, other direct costs.
5. Identify and budget work in work packages or planning packages.
6. Sum work package and planning package budgets to the control account budget.
7. Minimize, segregate, and control level-of-effort activity.
8. Establish overhead budgets at appropriate levels.
9. Identify Management Reserve and Undistributed Budget.
10. Sum Baseline Budgets and Management Reserve to the contract value.

Accounting Considerations

1. Record direct costs in Control Accounts.
2. Summarize direct costs by WBS without allocation to two or more WBS elements.

3. Summarize direct costs by OBS without allocation to two or more OBS elements.
4. Record and allocate indirect costs to the contract.
5. Identify costs of units or lots produced.
6. Record material costs upon receipt of material or later, on a basis consistent with budgets, providing full accountability of all material.

Analysis and Management Reports

1. Identify monthly, at the Control Account level, variances among Budget, Earned Value, and Actual Costs.
2. Identify monthly, differences between planned and actual schedule accomplishment.
3. Identity monthly, variances between budget and actual indirect costs.
4. Summarize all data by WBS and OBS.
5. Identify managerial actions taken to correct problems.
6. Update the Estimate of Cost at Completion.

Revisions and Data Maintenance

1. Incorporate contract changes in a timely manner.
2. Reconcile current baseline to original baseline.
3. Control retroactive changes to records.
4. Prevent revisions to the program budget except for authorized changes.
5. Document changes to the Performance Measurement Baseline.

Expressed in such explicit terms, the EVMSG and the EVMS guidelines requirements appear to be quite simple and basic. However, there are underlying requirements that have evolved over many years of determining acceptable and unacceptable contractor practices. These requirements are explained in the DoD Earned Value Management Implementation Guide. Therefore, some elaboration on the basic guidelines is in order.

Organization

To be considered acceptable, the WBS must be a product-oriented subdivision of the hardware, software, and services required by the contract. The government normally specifies the top three levels of WBS, which the contractor expands in accordance with the way the work will be done. The result is a single contract WBS that serves as the framework for planning, integrating, controlling and reporting work on the contract. A WBS Dictionary is required to describe the individual elements of work and to relate WBS elements to technical specifications, contract statements of work, project phases, funding categories, etc. Some negotiation of the government-specified WBS is possible, both before and after contract award, and care should be taken to make the final WBS as complete and logical as possible because it can be difficult to change the WBS during the performance of work and maintain an audit trail.

Identifying the organizations that will do the work to the individual elements of the WBS results in the formation of control accounts. The product of this exercise is a Responsibility Assignment Matrix (RAM) that illustrates the integration of the WBS with the OBS, including subcontractor participation. The size and duration of control accounts will have a large impact on the cost and effectiveness of system operation, making this determination a critical element of contract planning.

Integration of management subsystems (work authorization, budgeting, scheduling, accounting, estimating) is facilitated by the WBS and control account structure. As a minimum, subsystems must be integrated at the total contract and control account levels. A matrix for each major organizational element showing the key documents that authorize and control work, budget and schedule at the contract, control account and work package levels should be prepared to ensure that full integration exists.

The managers responsible for controlling indirect costs allocable to the contract must be identified with methods used for budgeting, control, and allocation of such costs clearly defined and documented.

The ability to accumulate data from the control account to the contact level through both the WBS and OBS without the need for allocations above the control account is also a requirement. The data reported to the government must be traceable back down either structure to the control account level.

Planning and Budgeting

At first blush, the EVMSG appear to be a little light in the area of scheduling. On closer examination, however, all of the fundamental requirements for a good scheduling system are included, without specifying the use of any particular scheduling methodology. All authorized work on the contract must be scheduled in a way that describes the sequence of work and identifies the significant task interdependencies required. The most commonly used scheduling technique that addresses interdependencies involves some form of networking. Yet the use of PERT, CPM, or other networking techniques is not prescribed. Modern schedule software is capable of employing network logic and presenting the output in the form of bar charts to facilitate its interpretation and use. The basic requirements are that a master schedule exists that covers the entire scope of work and which is supported by appropriate lower level schedules that are used to plan and control work activities. There must be no disconnects between the master schedule and the detail level schedules. The scheduling system must incorporate the development, production, and delivery requirements of the contract and must also identify technical performance goals, key milestones, output products, and other indicators of progress useful for measuring performance objectively. The system must also identify work achievement against the schedule plan, not simply revise the schedule plan as conditions change.

Perhaps, most importantly, the scheduling system cannot operate independently of other systems. In a cost performance measurement system, effective integration of budgets, schedules, and costs is essential to obtaining a clear picture of contact performance. The EVMSG baseline concepts require that such integration be established and maintained.

In order to measure contract performance, the baseline must represent the contract. This means that the budgets must add up to the contract value, and the schedule must be tied to contract milestones. If the baseline parts company with contractual goals, the system is no longer measuring contract performance. It is measuring something else. Such a departure can only occur if both contracting parties agree and understand the ramifications of the move.

Budgeting by cost elements (Labor, material, etc.) is required in order that cost variances can be analyzed in those terms. Labor and material cost are managed differently, and it is necessary to understand how much the total cost variance is attributable to each category, particularly in evaluating cost impact on the contract and for estimating cost at completion.

Work authorization must be done in a formal, documented manner, including the use of work authorizing documents to subdivide and assign work within control accounts. These documents also impose limitations on resource expenditures.

Ultimately, the work is broken down into work assignments through work packages and planning packages. The EVMSG require that performance measurement be determined based on work package accomplishments. Work packages are unique, identifiable, short-span units of work. Short-span is normally interpreted as about two accounting periods. Longer work packages must have objective indicators identified, scheduled, and budgeted to facilitate work-in-process measurement. Far term effort that cannot be work packaged within a control account should be identified in larger increments called planning packages. The concept of planning packages is intended to associate work with budget as soon as possible. Planning packages are subsequently broken down into work packages at the appropriate times. The sum of the budgets assigned to work packages and planning packages must equal the control account budget.

Where a contractor employs engineering or historical standards for measuring performance of workers, the budgets assigned to work packages must have a logical relationship to those values. Budget plans must also reflect anticipated efforts of "learning" gained through performance repetitive activities or processes. If work cannot be planned and measured in discrete terms, it may be classified as level-of-effort, but must be segregated from measurable effort, and its value earned based on the passage of time rather than on completion of activities.

Overhead budgets and costs must be managed in accordance with the contractor's cost disclosure statement using procedures acceptable to the Defense Contract Audit Agency. Management reserve and undistributed budget must be kept visible and all distributions reported to the government on the Cost Performance Report. Undistributed budget is regarded as a temporary holding account for budget that cannot be allocated to WBS or OBS elements at or below the reporting levels. The undistributed budget account should not contain large amounts of budget for long periods of time, or it may be viewed as a substitute for adequate contract planning. Except for unusual situations, undistributed budget should be allocated within two accounting periods, although budget for authorized, undefinitized work may remain until negotiations have been completed. Use of management reserve is regarded as a problem indicator and must be explained in terms of WBS and organizational elements to which it is applied, including the nature of the problem and outlook.

Accounting Considerations

The EVMS accounting requirements envision that direct costs will be recorded in control accounts and summarized, without allocation, to the contract level both by WBS and OBS. Indirect costs are allocated at the level selected by the contractor for control of such costs and summarized to the contract level. If apportioned effort is used, methods for applying such costs to control accounts must be documented and applied consistently.

The contractor's system must be able to accumulate the costs of completed units, equivalent units or lots as appropriate to the type of production involved. Segregation of recurring and nonrecurring costs should also be possible to support cost estimating for future procurements.

Accounting for material costs can be the most difficult and troublesome aspect of the accounting criteria because of the variety of materials involved and the different points in time when material accounting may occur. Material costs must be recorded in the same time period that value is earned for that material. The system must be able to distinguish between cost variances associated with the purchase price of the material separately from the variances attributed to excess usage of material. Material costs may be recorded as estimated actuals if earned value is determined at material receipt, even though actual costs do not enter the books of account until invoices are paid. Various categories of material may be treated differently; e.g., raw materials may not be accounted for until they are issued to work in process, even through they have been paid for earlier. Normally, costs may not be recorded for materials prior to the actual receipt of those materials. An exception would be where progress payments are being made to a vender based on evidence of physical progress leading to delivery of products.

Analysis and Management Reports

This is the section of the criteria that deals with performance measurement. Comparisons of key data elements (budget, earned value, actual costs) must be performed at the control account level and at higher levels as appropriate. Significant variances must be explored and corrective actions taken to compensate for cost and schedule problems.

Planned versus actual schedule accomplishment must be determined using indicators of physical progress compared to schedule plans. Results of this analysis should be reconciled to the schedule variances derived by comparing budget and earned value data.

Indirect budgets and costs must be compared at the levels identified for control of such costs, and significant variances identified. All direct and indirect data elements must be summarized for elements of the WBS and OBS to facilitate performance evaluation at higher levels and for reporting to the customer.

Information gleaned from these data collections and analyses must be disseminated to managers at various levels to ensure that it is available for use in management decision making and evaluating effects of corrective actions taken.

Based on actual performance trends, estimates of cost at completion must be updated and reconciled with funding requirements reported to the government.

Revisions and Data Maintenance

Keeping the baseline up to date and reflective of contractual provisions are essential prerequisites for good performance measurement. The EVMSG emphasize the need for timely, systematic incorporation of contract changes. If work is authorized to begin prior to negotiations, budgets must be established based on the contractor's estimated cost for that work. Current baseline budgets must be reconcilable to original budgets, and documentation must exist to show how adjustments were made.

Retroactive changes to records pertaining to completed work are prohibited except for corrections of errors or other adjustments agreed to by the procuring authority. Budgets must sum to the contract budget base (negotiated contract cost plus the estimate for authorized unnegotiated work) unless the contracting parties agree to establish a separate goal for management purposes (overtarget baseline).

Changes to the performance measurement baseline resulting from internal replanning must be reported to the government to ensure understanding of the effect of such changes. Changes to open work packages may be made under certain circumstances that are documented in written procedures.

Glossary of Terms

Actual Cost of Work Performed (ACWP): The costs incurred and recorded in accomplishing the work performed within a given time period.

Actual Costs: See Actual Cost of Work Performed (ACWP).

Apportioned Effort: Effort that by itself is not readily divisible into short-span work packages but which is related in direct proportion to measured effort.

Budget: An allocation of the total authorized budget/contract budget base or contract target cost to scheduled increments of work.

Budget at Completion (BAC): The sum of all periodic or incremental budgets (BCWS) planned to accomplish the specified work.

Budgeted Cost for Work Performed (BCWP): The sum of the budgets for completed work packages and completed portions of open work packages, plus the applicable portion of the budgets for level of effort and apportioned effort. Also referred to as earned value.

Budgeted Cost for Work Remaining: The budget at completion (BAC) minus the budgeted cost for work performed.

Budgeted Cost for Work Scheduled (BCWS): The sum of the budgets for all work and planned tasks, etc., scheduled to be accomplished (including in process work), plus the amount of level of effort and apportioned effort scheduled to be accomplished within a given time period.

Contract Budget Base (CBB): The negotiated contract cost plus the estimated cost of authorized unpriced work. Also known as total authorized budget.

Contract Target Cost (CTC): The negotiated cost in a fixed-price-incentive contract or a cost-plus-incentive contract, or the estimated cost in a cost-plus-fixed-fee contract.

Contract Work Breakdown Structure (CWBS): The complete work breakdown structure for a contract. The CWBS consists of the WBS specified in the contract plus the contractor's extension thereof to reflect the way the work will be performed.

Control Account: The control account is where program cost, schedule and work scope requirements are integrated, planned and managed. Resource planning through integration of schedule and budget objectives, and performance measurement will be accomplished within the control accounts.

Cost Performance Index (CPI): The average cost efficiency with which work has been performed. The CPI is derived by dividing the earned value by the actual costs.

Cost Variance (CV): The difference between earned value and actual costs derived by subtracting actual costs from earned value. A negative answer represents unfavorable cost performance.

Earned Value: The value of completed work expressed in terms of the budget assigned to that work. Also referred to as budgeted cost for work performed.

Estimated Actual Costs: The estimated cost of material that has been received but has not yet been paid for. Estimated actual costs are derived from purchase orders, invoices or other information, and can be used for performance measurement purposes until the actual costs are recorded in formal accounting records.

Estimated Cost at Completion (EAC): The actual costs incurred to date plus the estimated cost (direct and indirect) for all remaining work.

Indirect Costs: The cost incurred by an organization for common or joint objectives which cannot be identified specifically with a particular project or activity. Also referred to as overhead costs.

Level of Effort (LOE): Effort of a general or supportive nature which does not produce definite end products.

Management reserve (MR): An amount of the total allocated budget withheld for management control purposes rather than designated for the accomplishment of a specific task or set of tasks. It is not a part of the Performance Measurement Baseline.

Operating Budget: A budget authorization, separate from the Performance Measurement Baseline, which can be used for internal control purposes. Operating budgets are not included in earned value calculations.

Organization Breakdown Structure (OBS): The hierarchical arrangement for a company's management organization, graphically depicting the reporting relationships. Normally, the OBS is limited to showing only managerial positions, but may depict lower organizational levels.

Overtarget Baseline (OTB): Replanning of the effort remaining in the contract, resulting in a new budget allocation which exceeds the contract budget base.

Performance Measurement Baseline (PMB): The time-phased budget plan against which contract performance is measured. It is formed by the budgets assigned to control accounts and the applicable indirect budgets. For future effort, not planned to the control account level, the performance measurement baseline also includes budgets assigned to higher level CWBS elements and undistributed budgets. It equals the total allocated budget less management reserve.

Planning Package: A logical aggregation of work within a control account, normally the far-term effort, that can be identified and budgeted in early baseline planning, but is not yet defined into work packages.

Resource Leveling: Rephasing of scheduled activities to maximize the efficient use of available resources.

Responsibility Assignment Matrix (RAM): A graphic representation that reflects the integration of project participants (internal organizations, work teams, subcontractors) with individual WBS elements to form control accounts.

Rubber Baseline: The improper movement of baseline budget (BCWS) without movement of the associated work to reduce or eliminate variances.

Schedule Performance Index (SPI): A ratio of the value of work performed to the value of work scheduled. The SPI is derived by dividing the earned value by the budget.

Schedule Variance (SV): The difference between budget and earned value derived by subtracting budget from earned value. A negative answer indicates that less work has been accomplished than was planned; it may or may not represent a behind-schedule condition.

To Complete Performance Index (TCPI): The projected rate of value to be earned for every measurable unit consumed in the future. Frequently used as an independent check of estimates at completion quality. It is compared to the CPI.

Total Allocated Budget (TAB): The negotiated contract plus the estimated cost of authorized, unpriced work. the TAB will always equal the Contract Budget Base except if there is an Over Target Baseline (OTB). Also known as the as Contract Budget Base (CBB).

Undistributed Budget (UB): Budget applicable to project or contract effort that has not yet been identified to WBS or OBS elements at or below the levels designated for reporting performance to management or to the customer.

Value Milestone: An objective indicator within a work package that can be used for measuring progress of work and determining earned value. It has a described scope of work, accomplishment criteria, assigned budget, and schedule.

Work Breakdown Structure (WBS): A product-oriented family tree division of hardware, software, services, and other work tasks which organizes, defines, and graphically displays the product to be produced, as well as the work to be accomplished to achieve the specified product.

Work Package: Short-span jobs, or material items, identified for accomplishing work required to complete the project or contract. A work package has the following characteristics:

(1) It represents units of work at levels where work is performed.

(2) It is clearly distinguished from all other work packages.

(3) It is assignable to a single organizational element.

(4) It has scheduled start and completion dates and, as applicable, interim milestones, all of which are representative of physical accomplishment.

(5) It has a budget or assigned value expressed in terms of dollars, manhours, or other measurable units.

(6) Its duration is limited to a relatively short span of time or it is subdivided by a discrete value milestones to facilitate the objective measurement of work performed.

(7) It is integrated with detailed engineering, manufacturing, or other schedules.

Index

About the author . . .

Robert R. Kemps is the recipient of the Federal Government's Distinguished Career Service Award bestowed upon him by the Department of Energy in August, 1989. After 36 years of combined military and civil service, he retired at that time as the director of Project and Facilities Management for DOE, where he was responsible, since May of 1980, for department policies related to project and construction management, including the DOE Cost/Schedule Control Systems Criteria (C/SCSC).

For eleven years, Robert Kemps was the Department of Defense focal point for C/SCSC and related cost reporting requirements. He wrote and was a major contributor to DOD documentation during that period.

The author has been involved with development of project management practices for the federal government since the middle sixties. With his extraordinary talent and invaluable experience he published the first edition of *Fundamentals of Project Performance Measurement* while an engagement director with Humphreys & Associates, Inc. The latter is a management consulting firm specializing in integrated project management systems with its corporate office located in Orange, California.

Kemps retired from the U.S. Air Force in September, 1973, as a Lt. Colonel and Master Navigator after 20 years of military service, which included assignments at Headquarters Air Force Systems Command and in the Office of the Secretary of Defense. He served for six years as a member of the board of directors of the Performance Management Association, now the College of Performance Management.